LA BRIDE

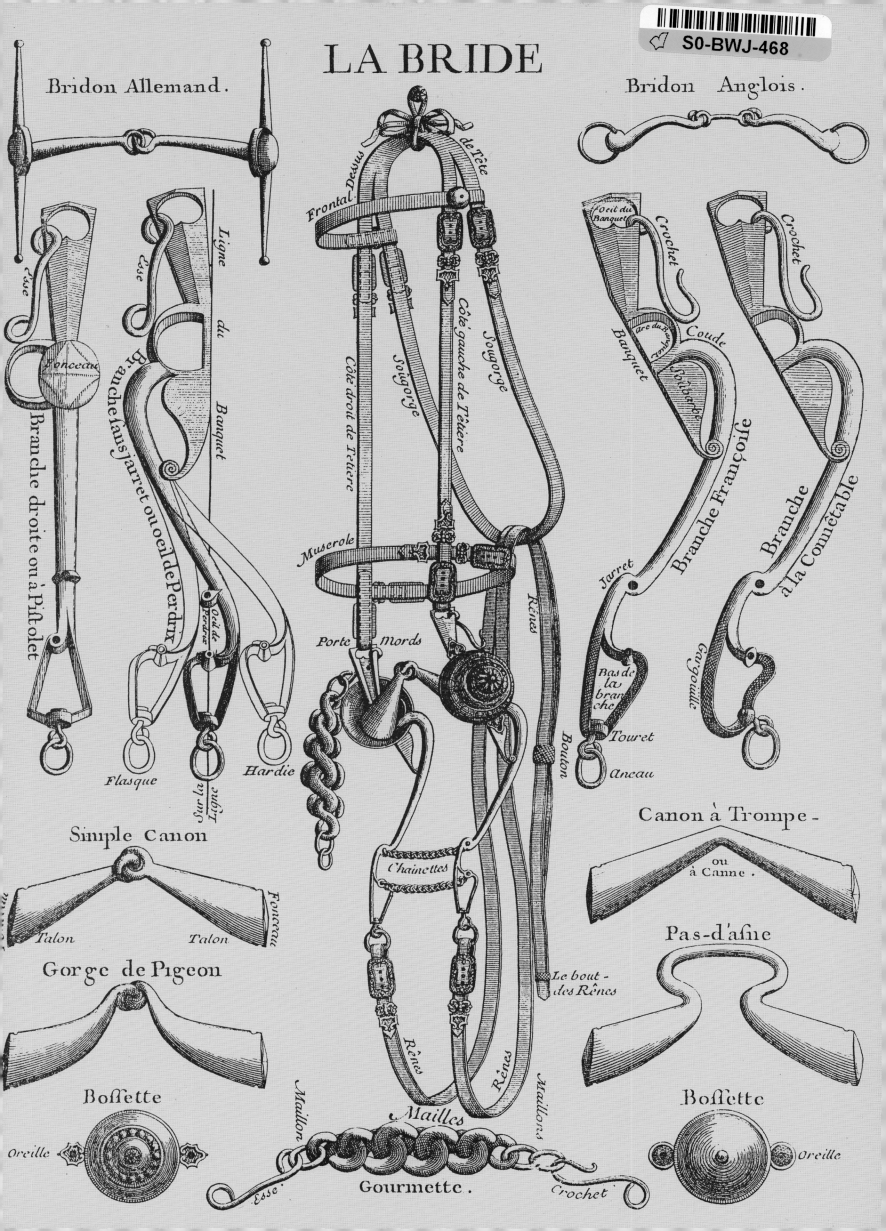

Bridon Allemand.

Bridon Anglois.

Esse

Esse

Ligne du Branche

Branche fausjarret ou oeil De Perdrix

Ponceau

Branche droite ou à Pistolet

Oeil de Perdrix

Sur la Ligne oubit

Flasque

Hardie

Frontal Dessus

de Tête

Côté gauche de Têtiere

Côté gauche de Têtiere

Soügorge

Soügorge

Côté droit de Têtiere

Muserole

Porte   Mords

Chainettes

Rênes

Rênes

Rênes

Maillon

Maillon

Maillons

Le bout - des Rênes

Oeil du Banquet

Crochet

Crochet

Banquet

arc du Banquet

Coude

Spilvare

Jarret

Bas de la branche

Touret

Aneau

Branche Françoise

Branche à la Connétable

Gargouille

Canon à Trompe - ou à Canne.

Pas-d'asne

Simple Canon

Talon

Talon

Fonceau

Gorge de Pigeon

Bossette

Bossette

Oreille

Oreille

Maillles

Esse

Gourmette.

Crochet

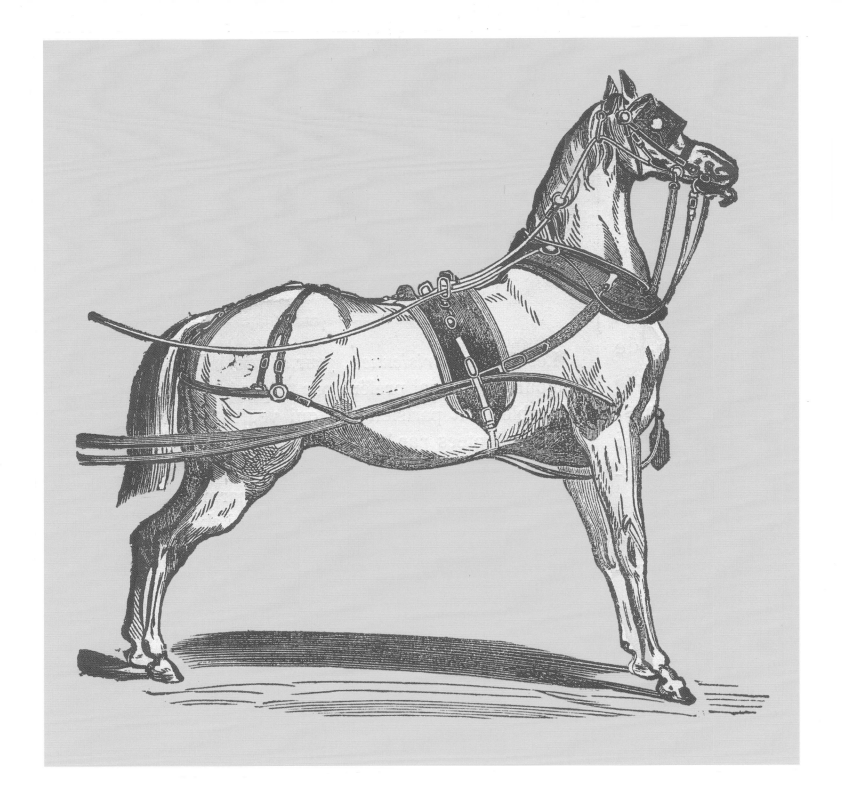

Front cover:
An eigtheen-year-old horse
Slide/Okapia/Lenz

Pages 2/3:
La Guérinière

Back cover:
The Cadre Noir de Saumur

Page 129:
Military bridle and harness of an officer of the Garde Républicaine

Photographic credits:

Slide/ACE: 53; **Slide**/Agraci: 112; **Slide**/Doumic: 106, 107; **Slide**/Durand: 13; **Slide**/Lade: 97, 110; **Slide**/Lemoine: 10, 24/25, 32/33, 37, 38/39, 41, 42/43, 47, 49, 54/55, 56/57, 58/59, 65, 89, 91, 103; **Slide**/Okapia: 1, 29, 44/45, 50/51, 60/61, 63, 64, 66/67, 100/101; **Slide**/Perrin: 109; **Slide**/Rainer Binder: 26/27; **Gros de Beler:** 16, 17; **B.N.:** 18/19, 20, 21, 22/23; **Morel/PSV/Konica:** 35, 83, 87, 94, 95; **Frédéric Dumas:** 85; **Min. Agr. Haras Nationaux of France/Annebique, D.R.:** 6/7, 31, 70/71, 72/73, 92/93; **E.N.E./Laurioux, D.R.:** 74, 76, 77, 78, 99, 136; **Garde Républicaine, D.R.:** 68, 81, 129; **D.R.:** 4, 14/15, 79, 82, 105, 130/131.

Contribution: Victor Siméon, F.B.

A CELEBRATION OF
THE HORSE

Foreword
Guy Baratoux

MOLIÈRE

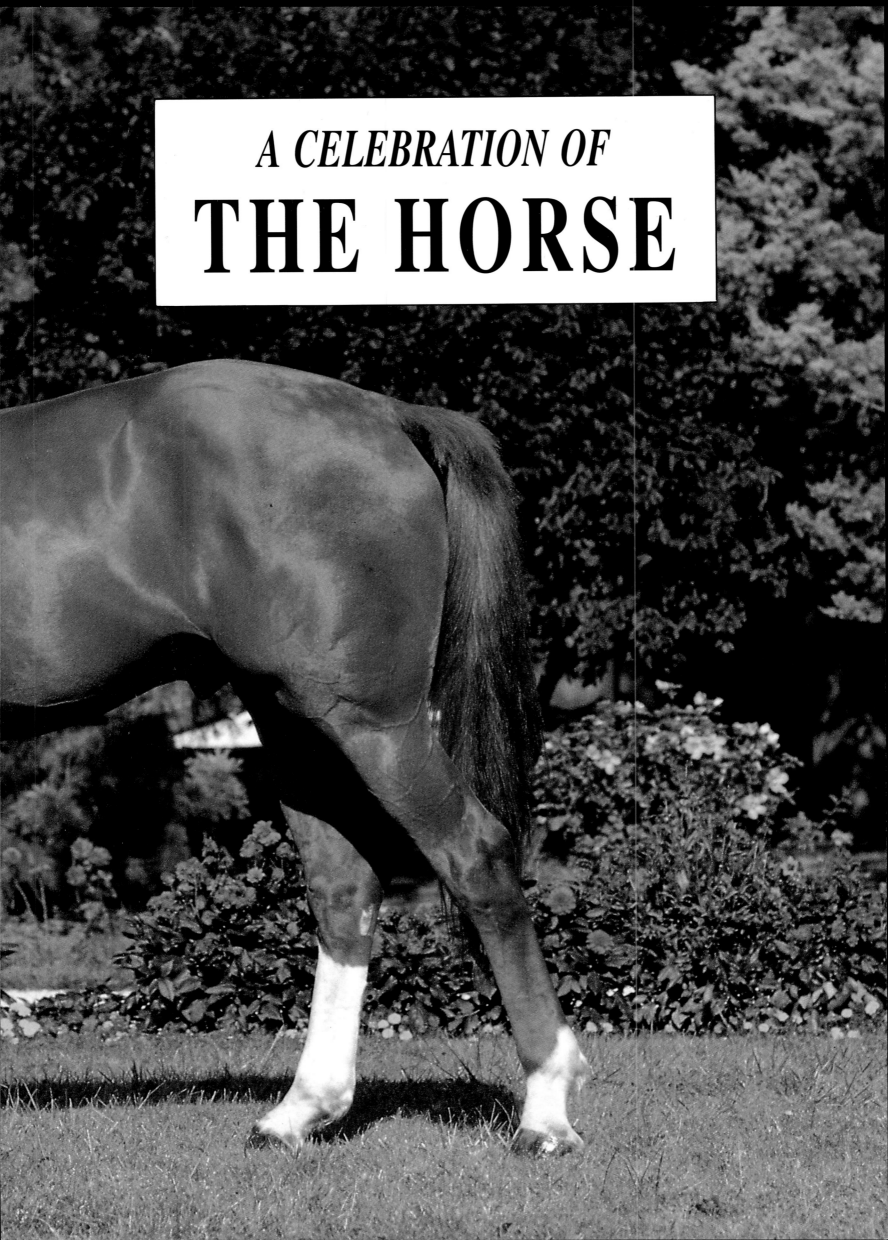

A CELEBRATION OF
THE HORSE

Haras Nationaux

FOREWORD

"My kingdom for a horse!"

Even though Richard III of England only uttered these words out of desperation in an attempt to save his own life, the phrase has become legendary, and what a legend, indeed! Is there any other animal that has been such an inspiration to poets, that has played such a role in history, that has been so essential in helping man become Man?

The great battle at Eylau, the taking of Somosierra Pass by Polish cavalry lancers of the Imperial Guard, the utter havoc at Balaklava would have been events of sheer folly without the horse. Thanks to the horse, such indescribable moments have become the stuff of dreams, enabling man to surpass himself.

Imagine the stag hunt without the horse. Imagine a landau pulled by four oxen. Imagine the legend of Napoleon without General Lasalle or Prince Murat. Imagine history without legend. Imagine the humdrum and the everyday. Or rather, do not imagine it!

Imagine instead those moments that make man the equal of the gods. Riding a horse at dawn, ambling through the dew... Or an autumn evening in the forest, listening for the hounds, on the trail of a deer... or simply, at night, stretched out beneath the stars, with your head on your saddle, peering through the campfire flames and seeing, silhouetted against the sky, the profile of the horse who brought you here. Then you will understand that there is man, there is the horse, and then there is all the rest.

"Nothing in the world is more beautiful than a galloping horse, a frigate in the wind or a woman dancing."

Only ladies, poets and men with the hearts of princes are worthy to mount a Thoroughbred.

Guy BARATOUX
Former Director
of the Haras National de Pompadour

CONTENTS

THE HISTORY OF THE HORSE

Ancestors

Looking over the genealogy of the horse, one notices that its earliest known ancestor, Eohippus, can be traced back to circa sixty million years BC. This animal was barely larger than a hare (12 inches), and had four toes on its front feet and three on its back feet. Eohippus lived in the forests and marshlands of North America and Europe and fed mostly on leaves and wild berries.

Over the centuries this ancestor of the horse underwent enormous changes, especially in size. To facilitate running, his only defense against predators, the central toe of each foot developed considerably, while the others, which no longer touched the ground, atrophied and eventually disappeared. All that remains in the modern day horse is a tiny callus-like growth on the inner surface of the foreleg known as a chestnut. Gradually the only remaining toe was transformed into a hoof. Thus, it took Equus, the true horse, sixty million years and several phases of development to come into being. A number of characteristics of prehistoric horses can still be found in the present day Przewalski's Horse or Asian Wild Horse. These small horses belong to an endangered wild breed that was discovered quite recently in Mongolia.

Before being domesticated, the horse was highly prized as game. Its power, speed and keen sense of smell, as well as its propensity to bite, kick, and fight, made it difficult prey to capture. The technique often used at that time was the battue, or beat, in which hunters would drive the herd into a cul-de-sac where the horses would be easier to kill. In the Maconnais region of France, horses were cornered at the top of Solutré Rock and became terrified and jumped off the cliff to their deaths. So many animal bones have been discovered at this famous prehistoric site that it has come to be known as the "*Cros* mass grave". Horse skeletons are the most numerous: there are estimated to be more than 100,000. These skeletons alone form a layer that is spread out over several acres and is a yard deep in places.

Horse flesh was highly prized as meat; horsehide was used for making certain articles of clothing, while horsebone was used for making tools that were sometimes finely carved. The other renowned site where these prehistoric hunts are represented is the Lascaux Caves, located in the Dordogne region of France. They were discovered in 1940 by four young people looking for their dog, which had disappeared into a hole. With the limited lighting at their disposal they spotted an extraordinary fresco painted on the walls of the cave. The famous prehistorian Abbot Breuil made extensive studies of these cave-paintings, which are considered the finest in Europe from this long-gone era. Drawings of horses are of primordial importance in the paintings, and an entire panel of the cave is devoted to them. Some could easily be mistaken for Przewalksi's Horses, like the Upside-down Horse, which is more delicate and higher on his feet. Several long-haired ponies are also depicted.

Domesticated since antiquity in Central Asia, the horse was imported into China, Western Asia, Europe and Africa during various migrations of nomadic herdsmen. If the oldest extant representation of a horse goes as far back as the Lascaux paintings, the oldest of a horse-drawn chariot, a bas-relief from Prinia in Crete, only dates as far back as 2000 BC. It was to take many long and perilous attempts before man succeeded in mastering the rudiments of harnessing and of horseback riding. It was in Dereivka,

The Lascaux Caves

A scale reproduction has been made of the Lascaux Caves near the famous Paleolithic site which is known as Lascaux II. The caves had been deteriorating badly due to the breath of visitors, but since 1984 visitors have once again been able to enjoy these frescoes, which were instrumental in revitalizing the study of prehistory. Among the many animals depicted in motion, horses play an important role.

Following pages
The horse family, or Equidae

This family of mammals is strictly herbivorous and has hooves at the extremities of its fore and hindlegs. Above left, a zebra (Hippotigris zebra); right, a domestic ass (Equus asinus); below left, a zebra-like quagga (Hippotigris quagga); right, an Arabian Horse (Equus Caballus).

in southern Ukraine, that the first traces of domestication were discovered: a four thousand year old bit carved out of deer antlers. The pieces of harnesses found during excavations prove that the first utilization of the horse was for hauling.

Before being used for riding, horses were long used harnessed to plows and to war chariots. At that time people must have had great difficulty capturing live horses. Presumably the first captive horses were young foals or pregnant mares destined to be eaten. Locked up in their enclosures these horses gradually became accustomed to humans. Their captors no doubt practiced selective breeding, keeping the most docile horses and slaughtering the more stubborn ones or those with skittish temperaments. Human beings had come to realize the many benefits the horse could offer them.

The first great horse breeders were certainly the Aryan peoples. In the 6th century BC the Persians were renowned for producing war horses as well as race horses and parade horses.

Above
**Karnak:
13th century BC, the
Great Temple of Amon**

*Seti I surrounded by Hittite
prisoners. Ramses II, his son,
completed the vast architectural
undertaking his father had
begun. Unlike their neighbors
and enemies, the Hittites and the
Assyrians, for the ancient
Egyptians the horse was more a
parade animal than a battle
animal.*

Facing page
Palace of Sargan II

*The elegance and finesse of
these two horses with Assyrian
style harnesses are remarkable.*

Antiquity

Frescoes can be found dating from as early as the 13th century BC representing warriors on their chariots; their heavy battle dress made frontal combat impossible. At that time the cavalry were most often used for intimidating and harassing the enemy and carrying out reconnaissance missions. The Hittites, the Assyrians and the Scythians were known for their outstanding cavalry. The Greeks and the Romans used infantrymen in waging war, so their cavalries were not very sophisticated. Nevertheless, it was a Greek, the General and historian Xenophon (430-355 BC) who wrote the most ancient equestrian treatises: "On Horsemanship" and "The Hipparchikos". Horses were brought from Sicily, Peloponnesus, Thessaly and Africa. In both Athens and Rome chariot racing was extremely popular. The Romans used submissive tribes for equestrian combat, such as the Numidians, Moors, Goths or Germans, as they were far more competent horsemen. They were therefore able to conquer the valorous Gaullic cavalry whose courage even Julius Caesar was forced to admire. During the decline of the Roman Empire the timid attempts at improving horse breeds through successive cross-breeding fell by the wayside. No progress was to be made in breeding until the arrival of the Capetians.

The Middle Ages to the Present

Although chivalry tournaments and the Crusades did indeed play a significant role in the Middle Ages, most films and portrayals of the era present a totally anachronistic image of the cavalry. At that time, fine, elegant horses were few and far between. The mounts were more likely to be draft horses used for plowing as well as in chivalry. This sturdy type of horse was necessary to withstand the weight of the knights with their heavy armor and the violent frontal shocks they sustained on the battlefield.

Selective and purposeful breeding would begin very hesitantly from the 11th century onward with the development of a rural economy. Heavy animals known as sumpter-horses were used for working the fields and as pack-horses, chargers were used for combat, and cobs for hunting and travel. There were, however, some lighter horses as well, such as the palfrey for parade, courtauds for pulling light horse-drawn chariots, and hackneys, which were used by ladies for travelling, as their gait is particularly comfortable.

The Arab invasions and the Crusades were to introduce much finer, lighter horses to the West. A large number of stallions were thus brought to Europe in order to improve the local breeds.

The appearance of firearms capable of piercing through breastplate armor was a determining factor in making the cavalry lighter. The cavalry were no longer to be used exclusively for violent frontal charges. Many kings, aware of the superiority of a light cavalry, began to legislate previously uncontrolled horse breeding. In England, Henry VII issued a decree forbidding horses under four feet tall to be used for breeding purposes. His successor, Henry VIII, established the height of stallions at five feet and decreed that all horses of inferior height be slaughtered. In France, Charles VII, after heavy losses sustained during the Hundred Years' War, also decided to create The Unattached Troop of Light Horses.

It was during the Renaissance, in their campaigns in Italy, that the French cavalry would evolve significantly as a result of the influx of eastern sires and the strong genetic changes they effected. In France real progress was made in horse breeding in 1665 when Colbert founded the first Haras Nationaux, the royal stud farms. These farms for royal stallions were entrusted to private hands for the methodic improvement of the French breeds. The breeders were given financial incentives for having their mares

Latin manuscript from Roman times

This "Commentary on the Apocalypse" dates back to the mid 11th century. It belonged to the Abbot of Saint-Sever. Its very colorful iconography is suggestive of the Arab influence on this region of south-west France near Spain.

18

covered. Less than twenty years later, in 1683, during the first Ottoman threat to Vienna, Captain Byerley brought back from battle the Arabian stallion which was to bear his name and would become one of the three founding sires of the English Thoroughbred breed. But the horse was also used in peacetime, for example in the post, or *positi* in Latin. The *positi* was a rapid messenger service in which horses were kept positioned in certain precise locations. This system of communication functioned throughout antiquity,

especially among the Persians. In 122 BC the *positi* put in place by the Romans covered all of Italy. The emperor Augustus extended it to the entire empire. To get news from outlying provinces, official dispatches were sent out along the Roman ways by cavalrymen, and later by relays of chariots. There were people stationed near these roads in charge of supplying the horses and ensuring their upkeep.

Louis XI reinstated these posts, positioning depots along all the kingdom's main roads where four or five horses would be available for use with the proper authorization. Around 1550, the post became a public service and users would pay a few cents to rent a horse. The French Revolution still maintained supreme control over the circulation of mail, but no longer over that of travelers. It was at this time that the large stagecoach companies were created. The nobility and the bourgeoisie utilized these horse-drawn carriages as well, which conferred a certain amount of

prestige upon them. In towns there was a lot of admiration for high quality equipment, and the gleaming harnesses and carriages made by well-known coach-builders came to be increasingly sought-after. Traffic in Paris was already becoming a problem, with stage-coaches, omnibuses, broughams, drays, landaus, and phaetons all vying for space on the roads.

When speaking of the history of the horse, it is essential to mention its enormous contribution to agriculture. For many centuries draft horses were the sole means of hauling and of transportation in the countryside. Horses did the plowing, sowing, harvesting and other work in the fields, and often represented peasants' only riches. As they were faster, horses succeeded in replacing oxen for furrowing, as well as for pulling barges and other types of vehicles. Until the end of the First World War, draft horses were widely used, but gradually the spread of mechanization in farming led to their decline.

The Golden Age: The Haute Ecole

Carousel given by the king in 1663

On a number of occasions equestrian festivals and carousels took place all throughout the long reign of Louis XIV. The court would try to distinguish itself through its skill and elegance.

The era of the light cavalry necessitated very specific training not only for the cavalrymen but for the horses as well. In 1532, in Naples, Federico Grisone founded the first martial equestrian academy. Nobles and officers from many countries came to become initiated in horsemanship. Very quickly the beauty of the figures used for battle and parade became evident.

They attempted to give more regularity and suppleness to the horse by creating artificial movements which were based on and enhanced natural attitudes, like the *passage* and the *piaffe*. Very soon this rather precious style of equitation became a favorite leisure activity of certain court nobles: the Haute Ecole, or High School, was born. It was introduced into France by Antoine de Pluvinel de la Baume who placed it under the protection of the Duke of Anjou, later to become Henri III. However, the golden age of the French Haute Ecole would begin under the Sun King, who had the Grand Stables of Versailles built by the architect Mansart.

The School of Versailles was created in 1680 and immediately became highly-reputed for its uncompromising quality and standards. In the 18th century, the director of the royal equitation school at the Tuileries, Antoine Robichon, known as La Guérinière, established the rules for equestrian academicism the world over, as well as the equestrian doctrine of the French School. After it was transferred to Austria, the Spanish Equestrian School created a charter delineating its principles and gave birth to the prestigious Spanish School of Vienna. The School of Versailles disappeared during the Revolution, to be replaced in 1796 by the very basic and short-lived School of Instruction of the Cavalry Troops.

It was to be one of the major weapons in the Napoleonic Wars. The cavalry's greatest victory was at Austerlitz, and its greatest defeat at Waterloo. During Napoleon's campaign in Egypt, he brought back a great variety of eastern stallions to improve the national bloodlines. Another disaster took place in 1870 at the battle of Reichshoffen. Mac Mahon led several mounted units to their deaths by ordering them to charge needlessly through the grapevines. In 1914, cavalry regiments still existed: the Spahis, Dragoons, Cuirassiers... Their uselessness during the war in the trenches and the massacre of the Russian and Polish cavalry regiments were to prove harbingers of the end of this invaluable weapon.

CHARACTERISTICS OF THE HORSE

Conformation

Horses are herbivorous mammals with uncloven hooves. They are social animals which in the wild generally live in plains and wide open pastures. Their body shape has slowly evolved throughout the centuries, to adapt to various different conditions and especially to their struggle against predators. Flight being their only defense, horses' physiognomy has altered to make them as fast as possible.

Essential to speed, horses' size has also changed throughout the ages. Today equines under 4.8 feet tall at the withers are considered to be part of the pony family, and those over this height are considered to be horses.

Intuitively, a lay person may often be able to judge the quality and health of a horse by considering the harmony of its conformation and the liveliness of its temperament. But this simplistic way of judging a horse is not sufficient; it is better to rely upon the expertise of professionals such as veterinarians, farriers or breeders who study precise aspects of beauty and defects of the animal. Nevertheless, before buying a horse or practicing horseback riding, a minimum knowledge of anatomy is necessary.

The body of a horse is divided into three parts: the forehand (the head, neck, withers and forelegs), the body (the back, chest and flank), and the quarters (point of hip, croup, buttocks, and hindlegs). Every breeder tries to bring out perfection in his or her particular variety of horse: that is, perfect adaptation of the horse's conformation to its future utilization. For jumping a horse should be supple and light, whereas driving in harness requires a heavier, more powerful horse with a broader chest.

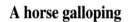

A horse galloping

Every anatomical detail has its importance. The equilibrium of the head and the neck is essential to the horse's balance and maneuverability. Excellent conformation allows a horse to jump over an obstacle correctly, and then to recover under the best conditions. The back is the most important element of impulsion for the hindquarters, and should be powerful and lightly sloped. The horse's equilibrium also depends upon the stand of the various limbs; knees, elbows, hocks, cannon bones, and pasterns should also be well proportioned. A horse whose hooves turn too far outwards is known as "wide in front," and one whose hooves turn too far inwards is called "narrow in front". Professional jargon such as "splay-footed," "sickle hocks," and "oxbow legs" describe various deformities or poor conformation of the limbs. The ideal conformation is when the limbs are perpendicular to the ground and neither spread too far apart nor too close to their median axis. Here the light conformation of this horse is perfectly suited to galloping.

Coats

There are two distinct categories of coats: whole or solid colored, in which the base coat and the hair are the same color, and colored or part-colored, in which there may be patches of various colors. Contrary to popular belief, true white coats are extremely rare; there must be no hair of any other color than that of the base coat. If even one black hair is found, it is enough to have a horse classified as a gray.

The same goes for black coats; a black coat must be immaculate: the bay brown does sometimes comes close however. The golden-brown coat with yellow and light beige hair in it constitutes one of the characteristics of the Palomino, most often found in the Americas than in Europa. Whether reddish-brown or fawn-colored, chestnut coats are by far the most common.

Colored or part-colored coats are most frequently made up of two different colors. There are those in which the base coat is one color and the outer hairs another, and those in which the colors are mixed. Horses belonging to the first category often have black manes and tails. Bays have reddish or dark brown hair, and grays, ash-gray hair.

The designation *isabelle* (black tale and mane and a dun-colored coat), dates back to the Crusades. It refers to Queen Isabeau of Bavaria who vowed she would never take off her blouse until her royal husband came back. By the time he finally returned, her beautiful white blouse had turned this yellowish-brown color. Among coats where the colors of the body and hair are mixed, there are red roans (white and reddish-brown body and hairs) and duns (reddish or yellow and

black base coat and hairs). One of the most highly-prized coat colors is gray, which is made up of white and black base coat and hairs and often comes close to white. This is the coat to be found on Camargues, certain Arabians and Lipizzaners. Horses with light geometric patterns on rather dark gray base coats are called dapple grays. There are also roans, with their reddish brown, white and black coats, and piebalds or skewbalds, which are quite common in the Americas and have coats with patches of two different colors. But chestnuts and bays are the most common. Certain characteristic markings (e.g. tufts, flesh marks, facial and muzzle markings, stockings,) give each horse its own distinctive appearance. All these details are noted in the stud book. Tufts are bunches of hairs growing against the grain of all the others. They can often be found on the forehead, chest and flanks. Flesh marks are hairless patches where the horse's skin can be seen, which is most often black. These areas can also

contain some pink unpigmented patches called marbled flesh marks. They are usually on the lips or at the tip of the nose. Easier to distinguish are facial and muzzle markings, the patches of white hairs on the forehead or running down the muzzle to the nose; these markings may sometimes join together. There is a very precise terminology for describing these markings, depending upon their specific appearance, size and direction.

Facial markings may be described using such terms as stars, round stars or half-moon stars, and may be located at the peak of the forehead, to the right or left, and may be oriented at an angle or crosswise. There is also a panoply of equally precise terms for qualifying muzzle markings. Leg markings are also patches of white hair and are to be found on the lower limbs. Depending on how high up they extend, they are known as white coronets or ermine marks, pasterns, socks or stockings.

A very wide variety

Looking at this herd at pasture, it is easy to see the wide range of equine coats. Here there are four varieties of gray coats and two bay brown foals; no one can guess what the bay browns' adult coats will look like. But the hair of horses, like that of humans, turns white with age.

The senses, sleep and intelligence

Whinnying allows a mare to call her foal back if he strays too far away, or an isolated horse to locate the rest of the herd by the response he receives. A worried horse will give out little snorts, as will a stallion if he is shown a mare. The sense of smell also plays an important role, and it is thanks to her sense of smell that a mare can recognize her foal. From the first moments of life, she takes in his odor by sniffing and licking him. From that point on it is very difficult to get her to adopt another foal. The sense of smell also enables a stallion to recognize a mare in heat.

Hearing is also very highly developed in horses. Horses are very sensitive to intonation. Dressage is done with the help of the voice, as horses' auditory memory is extremely well-developed. A horse can easily understand spoken orders. A precise, energetic order is often sufficient to get him back on the straight and narrow path. Reactions to the voice are particularly useful for harness and plow horses.

Many coachmen or team drivers lead their horses using only their voices most of the time. The same holds true for farmers and foresters, who although they need both hands for their work, still have to lead their horses for ploughing or clearing felled wood. In the old days a teamster only had to call out, "gee-ho!" for his horses to go forward or turn right, "haw!" to turn left, and a long, drawn out "whooooah!" for them to stop.

Lastly, it is through the sense of touch that horses show affection for one another; it is also the way horse and rider become as one. Feeling the contact of the rider's leg against him and the delicate way the rider's hands manipulate the reins, the horse regulates his speed and impulsion and lets himself be guided.

Watchful sleep

Almost constantly aware of what is going on around him, the horse only falls asleep for short splintered periods of time and remains standing most of the time. Alone in his meadow, he is thus able to remain vigilant. He only very occasionally lies down to sleep, unless he feels particularly safe or other horses in the herd are there to keep watch over his surroundings. Then some horses will take long naps stretched out in the sunshine. Horses, like humans, have three distinct phases of sleep: a drowsy, half-waking state, deep sleep and paradoxical sleep when, although the mysteries of the horse's subconscious have yet to be elucidated, it is not unreasonable to believe the horse dreams.

Is the horse an intelligent creature?

The intelligence of the horse is the subject of much debate. Some nay-sayers think horses are fundamentally stupid animals while others believe horses capable of real reflection. The horse is above all instinctive and intuitive. All his actions and reactions spring from his natural, sociable behavior, which mankind has learned to adapt for his own purposes. Thus, in the High School, in dressage and in circuses, a horse can be made to rear up or do figures like *croupades* and *caprioles*, which are essentially defensive reflexes. In horseracing it is the flight instinct which impels a horse to run.

The horse does, however, surprise us at times, for example, by showing great dexterity in unlocking his stall. There is the story of a pony which, after having gallivanted around outside his stall, proceeded to take mischievous pleasure in letting all his companions free too. Often when a rider loses his way, all he has to do is let himself be guided by his horse to find the way back to the stable.

In by-gone days fairs used to have horses on exhibit which were supposed to be able to count. They would do addition, giving the answers to the sums by stomping their hooves on the ground a certain number of times. Researchers have explained that this phenomenon is due to the horse's highly developed sense of intuition or telepathy. The horse is very sensitive to the mounting anxiety and nervous tension in the crowd when the time comes for him to stop stomping his hoof. The horse can also immediately sense the psychological state of his rider. If the rider is afraid, the horse always seems to take advantage of the situation to do as little work as possible; for example, refusing to budge when it is time to do exercises in the ring.

A very expressive head

Horses have a whole system of codes for communicating among themselves using their senses of touch, smell, sight and hearing. Every horseman and woman should become familiar with these codes to stay alert to his or her horse's psychological state. The ears of a horse are very sensitive and move about in every direction, much like semaphores. A horse will show his discontent or ill-humor by laying his ears back or threatening to kick or throw his rider. If however, his head is held high with the ears pricked up, it means he is paying particular attention to what is going on around him, and to what he is being told.

Paces

Until the 19th century, the exact mechanisms involved in horses' different paces were unknown to man. Many pictorial representations of horses in motion were fantastical, to say the least.

In the 1880's, professor Etienne Jules Marey took chronophotographic images which made it possible to deconstruct the action of a horse in motion for the first time. A horse's most common paces are the walk, trot, canter and gallop. There are other gaits, whether natural or artificial, such as the amble, the disunited canter, the tölt and the running walk.

Walk

The walk is the slowest, most natural pace in which part of the horse's body is always in contact with the ground. Diagonally the walk can be broken down into four beats. The left hindleg is lifted then touches down, then the hoof falls are left foreleg, then right hindleg, followed by right foreleg, and then back to the left hindleg. Depending on the impulsion the rider gives the horse or the will of a horse at liberty, the speed may vary. It is the pace which puts the least strain on the horse. Sometimes attaining a speed of four or five miles per hour, a horse can walk for four or five hours on end without becoming tired.

Trot

Just as natural is the trot, which is an intermediary pace between the walk and the gallop. The trot is a springing pace which can be broken down into two beats, in which the horse remains in suspension for an instant in between two beats. Two diagonal legs, such as the left foreleg and the right hindleg touch the ground simultaneously, creating impulsion, then come the right foreleg and left hindleg.

Racehorses are taught to be able to trot as quickly as possible without breaking into a gallop. They have to go through special training, in which they are reined in a special way and their shoes are sometimes even weighted down. Every year there are new records set for speed, like that of the seven year-old trotter Mister Lucken. He broke every existing world record at the great Cagnes Criterium race on March 10, 1991 when he covered a distance of 1609 meters in 1 minute 12.4 seconds. While in the "sitting trot" the rider remains in the saddle, the English style of riding predominant in Europe advocates the slightly faster "rising trot" in which the rider rises up on his stirrups and thus avoids being shaken.

Gallop

The gallop, the fastest pace, is certainly the most impressive, and contrary to what beginners usually assume, it is also quite comfortable.

This springing pace can be broken down into three beats followed by a moment of full suspension. During a gallop leading on the right, the impulsion is first given by the left hindleg, then by the left foreleg, the right hindleg and finally the right foreleg. A very brief instant during which the horse does not come into contact with the ground at all comes next. The maneuver is exactly the opposite for a left gallop. When moving in a circular trajectory a horse galloping correctly moves counter-clockwise for a right-handed gallop and clockwise for a left-handed gallop. It is always exhilarating to see a galloping herd of Camargues skimming through the sea foam with their manes streaming in the wind, a lofty dressage horse or a racehorse who seems to fly and just graze the ground. On the racetrack some horses can gallop over 43 miles per hour.

Jumping over obstacles

Whether of his own volition or during a competition, to jump over an obstacle a horse must have enough impulsion. Before jumping, the number of the horse's strides and his speed must be carefully controlled. Herein lies the greatest difficult in show-jumping. The rider must regulate the pace of his horse, holding him back enough and then letting him go at just the right time. As he approaches the obstacle at a trot or a gallop, the horse first raises his forequarters, then by extension of his hindlegs he projects himself off the ground. He then flies through the air and

recovers with a balancing motion of the head, neck and forelegs. He lands with head and neck held high so that his weight does not propel him forward. The outstretched forelegs touch ground first. When foals play they often jump over fences and natural obstacles that are to be found in their pasture. Jumping is not, however, entirely innate and a horse must undergo a long period of training before entering show-jumping competitions.

Specialized gaits

Horses must sometimes adopt more unusual or specific gaits, whether naturally or because they are forced to do so. An example is the amble, which was greatly appreciated during the Middle Ages for its comfort, especially by horsewomen who rode side-saddle, with both legs on the same side of the saddle. The amble is still common in South America, in the United States, in Iceland and in South Africa.

This two-beat "walked" gait in which the legs move together in lateral pairs is among the most comfortable. It can be passed down from generation to

generation, but is most commonly taught artificially by breaking a foal at a very young age. In the United States, harness racing is not done at a trot but at an amble whose mechanical regularity makes it possible to attain much greater speeds. It also significantly reduces the risk of injury to the horse.

Much less common is the disunited canter in which the horse gallops with its forelegs and trots with its hindlegs. It is often considered a defective gait, as horses nearing the end of their careers often use it when they have balance problems. Certain horses, like the Icelandic pony, use the tölt. The tölt is a four beat gait that is considered the most comfortable of all. Often only one hoof at a time touches the ground, which reduces shaking to a minimum.

The running walk is a gait particular to the Tennessee Walking Horse: the horse is made to raise his limbs extremely high. The running walk is obtained through artificial means often frowned upon by horse lovers: a chain is attached to each pastern with wooden wedges raising the hooves, which is very uncomfortable for the horse and forces him to walk this way.

A horse trotting

This is the pace best suited for judging the beauty and suppleness of a horse in motion. Average speed is estimated at 9 mph. This was the speed of stagecoaches on good roads.

BREEDS

Natural Evolution

A breed is a group of the same species whose members all share certain hereditary features. Different natural habitats have influenced and contributed to the formation of the various breeds of horses. For instance, the arid land of the Shetland Islands in the north of Great Britain, with its difficult climatic conditions, gave birth to extremely rugged little ponies, whereas the horses native to the pastures of Normandy are much larger and slender in form.

Humans beings, too, made important modifications to the various indigenous breed through repeated cross-breeding of their native horses with foreign animals. Gradually, through selective breeding, they managed to create a new style of animal, improving certain functional characteristics.

Draft horses, for example, are well-suited to working the fields, and lighter horses are better suited for riding or for pulling horse-drawn vehicles. Arabians and Thoroughbreds therefore became highly prized for improving indigenous breeds. They have contributed to refining and creating completely new breeds of horses: Anglo-Arabs, Trotters, Selle Français, Boulonnais, etc. As their renown increased, many of these horses began to be bred all over the world. True Thoroughbreds or Arabians can therefore be found on every continent.

Many breeds have a their own register, called a Stud Book, where their pedigrees are documented and the ascendance of a horse belonging to that breed can be verified. When a horse of unknown origin is accepted into a stud book because of the qualities it can contribute to the breed, we say that the book is open. If it is impossible to add a horse whose descendants do not already figure in the stud book, this is known as a "closed book". This is the case for the Thoroughbred.

A Thoroughbred

The English Thoroughbred is the epitome of a pure-bred, which is why in the profession it is simply known as the Thoroughbred, while the pure-bred is known as the Arabian.

The Arabian

The Arabian is considered to be the purest breed of horse. Its purity of line and elegance have earned it the monikers "gazelle" or "hare of the desert". It is an animal that has almost been deified, and has its place in the Koran. Islamic tradition holds that the Arabian horse is a descendant of Mohammed's five favorite mares, who arrived first in Mecca among the eighty-five horses the prophet sent to announce his victory. Legend also has it that the Arabian is a descendant of the seven founding sires selected from among King Solomon's 45,000 harness horses and 12,000 saddle horses. It is surprising that a horse whose appearance is so delicate and refined can also be so rugged and strong.

This proud horse of sultans is used to the difficult conditions in the desert and is renowned for its resistance and frugality. It has always been the companion of nomadic Middle Eastern peoples and shared in their lives. Nowadays Arabians are often used for competing in endurance races in which they must maintain an even pace for forty or fifty miles. Arabians, according to some specialists on the breed, can be divided into three distinct families: the Kheilans, with their light gray coats which are considered the most rugged, the elegant and pure Seglawis, and the more slender Munigi, which are by far the fastest.

The superiority of the Berber cavalry over that of the Crusaders contributed to their importation into Europe. A number of other historical events such as the Saracen invasions and the Napoleonic Wars only served to increase this tendency. The horses of Poland, Hungary, the former Soviet Union, Germany, and the Americas also underwent the positive influence of the eastern bloodlines. In France this cross-breeding created the Anglo-Arab breed. Most draft horses like the Percheron and the Boulonnais have benefited from Arabian blood as well. Thoroughbreds are also direct descendants of the three famous Arabian stallions. Pure-bred Arabians are treated like real stars, and not only because of their relatively recent utilization in endurance racing

where they are truly outstanding. The stud farms in North Africa are like palaces and the horses there are deeply venerated.

The character and fieriness of the Arabian are marvelously shown off during fantasias. These cavalry charges take place under the pounding heat of the midday sun amid clouds of dust. Superbly harnessed horses surge toward the crowd at full gallop while their riders execute spectacular combat maneuvers, shooting and reloading their carved shotguns called mokhalas, throwing them up into the air, then catching them in acrobatic positions and screaming wildly.

The fantasia originates in ancient war techniques used in North Africa for harassing the enemy. The warriors of the Maghreb would charge thunderously toward the enemy, then suddenly screech to a halt, shoot arrows at them and beat a retreat as quickly as they had come. In Arabic, this storming attack is known as *el kaar*, and the retreat *el farr*. Before the advent of rifles, Berber and Arab cavalrymen usually used crossbows. Every year the city of Meknes in Morocco holds a very famous fantasia festival. Over two weeks a huge number of horsemen divided into teams or *sorbas*, try to outdo one another for their skill and imposing bearing. In addition to Arabians, they also ride Barbs, the other steeds of the desert, which are just as rugged but of less noble and pure origin.

In the West, Arabians participate in the big gait class shows. With their coats impeccably groomed and shining, they are presented in-hand, standing, walking, and trotting. A further test at liberty also sometimes comes next. The jury notes the various evolutions of the horse left on his own either in a ring or arena. A test in costume with oriental costumes and harnesses ends this type of event. Over the past few years this type of competition has gained in popularity in Europe as well. Every year an Arabian world championship is organized in Paris as part of the Horse Fair.

The most beautiful head

The Arabian stands out from other horses due to its small size (14.2-15 hands high) which makes for a remarkably well-balanced horse. Arabians are very light and rarely weigh more than 900 pounds. The shape of the body and legs fit into a perfect square. The forehead and nose are wide, the large eyes are outlined by an area of darker hair that looks like eyeliner. The nostrils are wide and open and enable him to breathe very freely. The fineness and easy motion of the ears are expressive of the Arabian's great liveliness, force of character and attentiveness to what is going on around him. But it is the characteristic slightly inwardly curved line of his nose which defines the purity of the pure-bred Arabian.

The English Thoroughbred

As its name suggests, the English Thoroughbred originally comes from England. But nowadays it is more commonly referred to as the Thoroughbred, as it is now bred all over the world.

As early as the late 17th century, the British cross-bred indigenous mares with Oriental stallions. Forty-two of the kingdom's finest mares were chosen, grouped together and dubbed the Royal Mares. Then the three famous Arabian pure-bred sires Byerley Turk (1684-1690), Darley Arabian (1700) and Godolphin Arabian (1730) were imported. The result was the birth of this breed that is now so greatly revered by racegoers as the uncontested star of the racetrack.

This is the story of Godolphin Arabian: the King of Morocco gave him to Louis XV; he was then given to a simple carriage driver and water carrier who used him as a work horse. In France he was noticed by lord Godolphin, from whom he got his name. He was brought to England where he was used as a "teaser", i.e. put among the mares to determine when they were in season. By accident one of the brood-mares became impregnated, and the offspring was such a superb specimen that Godolphin became one of the founding sires of the Thoroughbred breed.

Descending directly from this cross-breeding, Herod, Eclipse and Matchem are equally well-known. Eclipse, who was born during the 1764 eclipse, was never beaten on the racetrack.

As Godolphin always finished several yards ahead of his competitors, they became discouraged and eventually gave up racing against him. He gave simple demonstrations of his prowess running alone. His phenomenal performance gave rise to such envy in the racing world that his owner began to receive anonymous death threats. Eclipse only raced for two years, whereupon he ended his career and proceeded to sire prestigious offspring. England and Ireland were indeed the birthplace of the breed, but today the United States has the largest number of Thoroughbreds and France has a solid reputation as well.

From these three great Eastern branches English breeders managed to create the fastest breed of horses in the world. Cross-breeding animals whose origins are very close does incur the risk of consanguinity, but this risk becomes negligible when a widely varied brood-mare base is used.

Criteria for height and rapidity have played as great a role in selective breeding as ancestry. In order to be recorded in the Thoroughbred stud book, a horse's ancestry must be irreproachable.

The English Thoroughbred is a race horse whose essential characteristic is a very aerodynamic anatomy. High on his hindquarters, he has a fine, noble head, and a long neck, shoulders and croup. His back is rather short and his gait supple, with extended low action. Thoroughbreds almost always have dark coats, and gray or light colored coats are quite rare. At eighteen months a Thoroughbred can begin his training as a race horse. The trainer is in charge of breaking the horse in, which is done in three weeks to a month. Now he can begin the horse's training in earnest. First he must gradually build up the horse's musculature, then work on his breathing and psychological condition in order to turn him into a true athlete capable of surpassing his competitors both in speed and in distance.

Training can be done either in private training facilities or places like racing clubs, racetracks, or in loose boxes and barns. There is an entire staff of qualified people under the trainer's orders, such as stable-boys to groom and ride the horse during training, and the first boy who is responsible for running the stable.

Training a galloping horse is usually done very early in the morning to avoid harm from the heat and sun. The trainer leads the session and follows the progress of each horse. Each session includes several different phases of exercises: first a rather long period of walking, so the horse can gently warm up his muscles before going out onto the track, then a trotting period to develop his muscles, and finally, he gallops with varying degrees of intensity and speed depending on how much time is left before the horse races are held. Then the trainer decides, based on the physical condition of the galloper, which races the horse should enter to win.

A stallion rearing

The physiognomy of the Thoroughbred has gone through enormous changes as a result of efforts to improve its genetic characteristics. Originally of a height of 14.6 hands, it can now be over 17 hands high. Its family bloodlines are very tightly controlled.

The Anglo-Arab

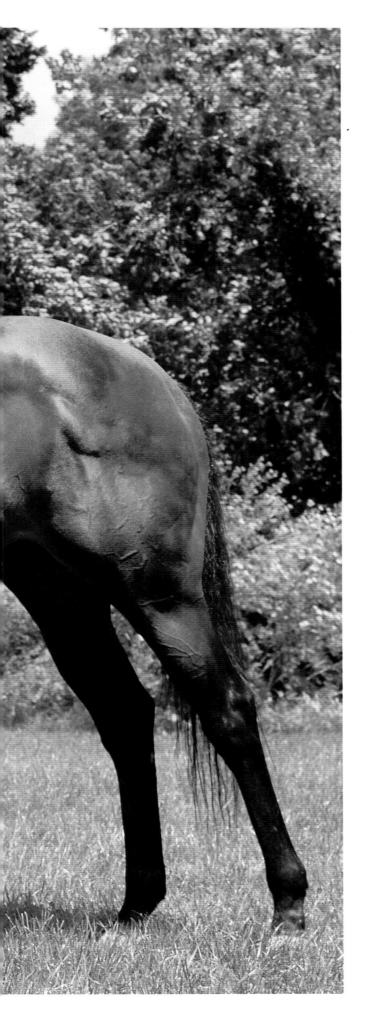

The Anglo-Arab breed comes from cross-breeding Thoroughbreds with Arabians. Although they have indeed been mated elsewhere, this breed essentially comes from France, mostly from the Southwest. It was created relatively recently, in the 1800s, during the time when the French were infatuated with all things English, known as anglomania. From 1818 on, a number of stallions were imported into France from England. The Duke of Cars at the La Source stud farm in the Sarthe region founded the first line from an Eastern stallion and the English mare Hirondelle. But it was a certain Mr. de Bonneval, the director of the Pompadour stud farm from 1815 to 1818, who is considered the true founder of the breed. He cross-bred the famous Arabian stallion Massoud with the two Thoroughbred mares Selim Mare and Deer. He was also responsible for mating the Turkish stallion Aslan and the British mare Comus Mare whose offspring was Cloris, one of the breed's founding sires.

Some breeders were so suspicious about the wisdom of this cross-breeding that it nearly put an end to the whole undertaking. The Anglo-Arab owes its survival to the efforts of Mr. Gayot, the veterinarian and then director of the Haras Du Pin stud farm. His idea was the systematic and large scale cross-breeding of the offspring of Arabians and Thoroughbreds. The objective was to thus obtain a horse much like both prestigious forefathers but more powerful and less fragile. Mr. Gayot was called to the Pompadour stud farm three years later and proceeded to transfer all his horses there, and gave them the name Pur-sang Français (French Pure-breds). He continued to do selective breeding at Pompadour, not with local breeders but with pure-bred English and Arab stock. The outstanding athletic performance of these horses that came out of Gayot's cross-breeding finally convinced other breeders. Anglo-Arabs began to be bred with one another from then on and the breed was officially recognized as such in 1860. Since 1880, only horses with 25% Arab blood whose forerunners are Thoroughbreds, Arabians or Anglo-Arabs have been accepted. The stallion Prisme (1890-1917) became one of the founding sires of the breed, siring more than fifty-eight stallions of extremely high quality.

An excellent sporting horse

Since 1965, the Anglo-Arab has been registered in the Selle Français stud book. Its conformation makes it an excellent galloper, although no rival to the Thoroughbred. It does have a certain advantage over other horses in non pure-bred races however. Anglo-Arabians are rarely more than 16 hands high and, thanks to their ancestors, have harmonious proportions and fine skin, but most of all they are surprisingly well-balanced, with lofty, well-extended gaits. The Anglo-arab's skill and endurance in jumping make it greatly appreciated in cross-country or combined training trials, also called eventing. The Anglo-Arab also stands out in all the other equestrian disciplines, such as harness-racing, dressage, jumping, hunter trials, and endurance riding. Certain show-jumping riders criticize the Anglo-arab's short height, but this handicap is largely compensated for by its exceptional drive, willingness to meet every challenge and perfect sense of balance.

The Selle Français

The Selle Français is one of the breeds formerly known as half-breds, that is the fruit of cross-breeding between pure-breds and indigenous horses. The term has been deemed too pejorative compared to *pure-bred* and is rarely used nowadays. The Selle Français is also the direct descendant of the half-bred lines that were once bred in France as carriage horses or saddle horses.

Several varieties of half-breds, such as the Anglo-Norman horse were to prosper all over France. The Vendéen, Charentais, Breton, Angevin and half-breds from central France, and from the Ain and Charolais regions have been recognized as well. The decree of December 18, 1958 groups all these bloodlines together under the name Selle Français. The physical attributes of this horse, along with its docility, endurance and spirit make it an excellent horse for leisure riding as well as competitions; consequently, most French equestrian centers boast this type of horse.

As they were responsible for improving the breed, the Haras Nationaux (French national stud farms) started selecting reproducers very early on; these horses were chosen not only for their conformation but also for their aptitude and performance in jumping competitions. Sires and brood-mares were rated and given a selection index based on their forerunners and their offspring.

Great Selle Français and Thoroughbred stallions have been instrumental in creating and refining the breed, among them such note-worthy sires as Ibrahim, Uriel, Jalisco B, Almé, Grand Veneur, Furioso, Rantzau, and Ultimate. Foals by a father belonging to the above-mentioned breeds and a mother who is a trotter are also registered in this stud book.

Faced with tough competition abroad, Selle Français have succeeded, especially over recent years, in imposing and demonstrating their impressive qualities on racetracks the world over. Thanks to horses such as these and their excellent riders, France managed to rise to European show-jumping champion in 1987 and 1991 and world champion in 1990 (gold medallist Quito de Baussy ridden by Eric Navet, and bronze medallist Morgat ridden by Hubert Bourdy). Horsemen from the 1980's and 90's will never forget the marvelous epic of Jappeloup, who challenged the world's greatest horses with Pierre Durand in the saddle, and won prestigious victories for France, such as Olympic champion in solo and group competition in Seoul in 1988.

This extraordinary record of achievements raises debate on the correlation between the size of a horse and its skill in jumping over large obstacles. For, although certain riders particularly like large horses (some Selle Français can be more than 16 hands high at the withers), Jappeloup was famous for his short stature, which tends to prove that shorter horses entrusted to excellent riders can be just as brilliant.

A horse with quite varied bloodlines

As a result of the diversity of its ancestors, there is really no precise standard for the Selle Français. Nonetheless, it can be said that the Selle Français stands relatively tall: sometimes more than sixteen hands high and is very powerfully built. Selle Français horses have substance, that is, solid skeletal structure and good general musculature.

Non Pure-breds

Non Pure-breds, or AQPS as they are known in French, (Autre Que Pur Sang,) are horses that are the product of a cross between a Thoroughbred stallion and a Selle Français mare "with very close blood" or an Anglo-Arab mare. It is not a separate breed, but rather a professional designation. The forerunners of these horses have passed down an overall aptitude for all equestrian disciplines as well as great success in flat-racing and obstacle racing. On Parisian racetracks like Auteuil and Longchamp, during the famous Prix de Craon, but also in the provinces in races open to them, it is not unusual to see certain non pure-breds outrun the Pure-breds. Therefore, many small owners who don't have the means to own and train Thoroughbreds but are just as passionate about horses and racing own this type of horse.

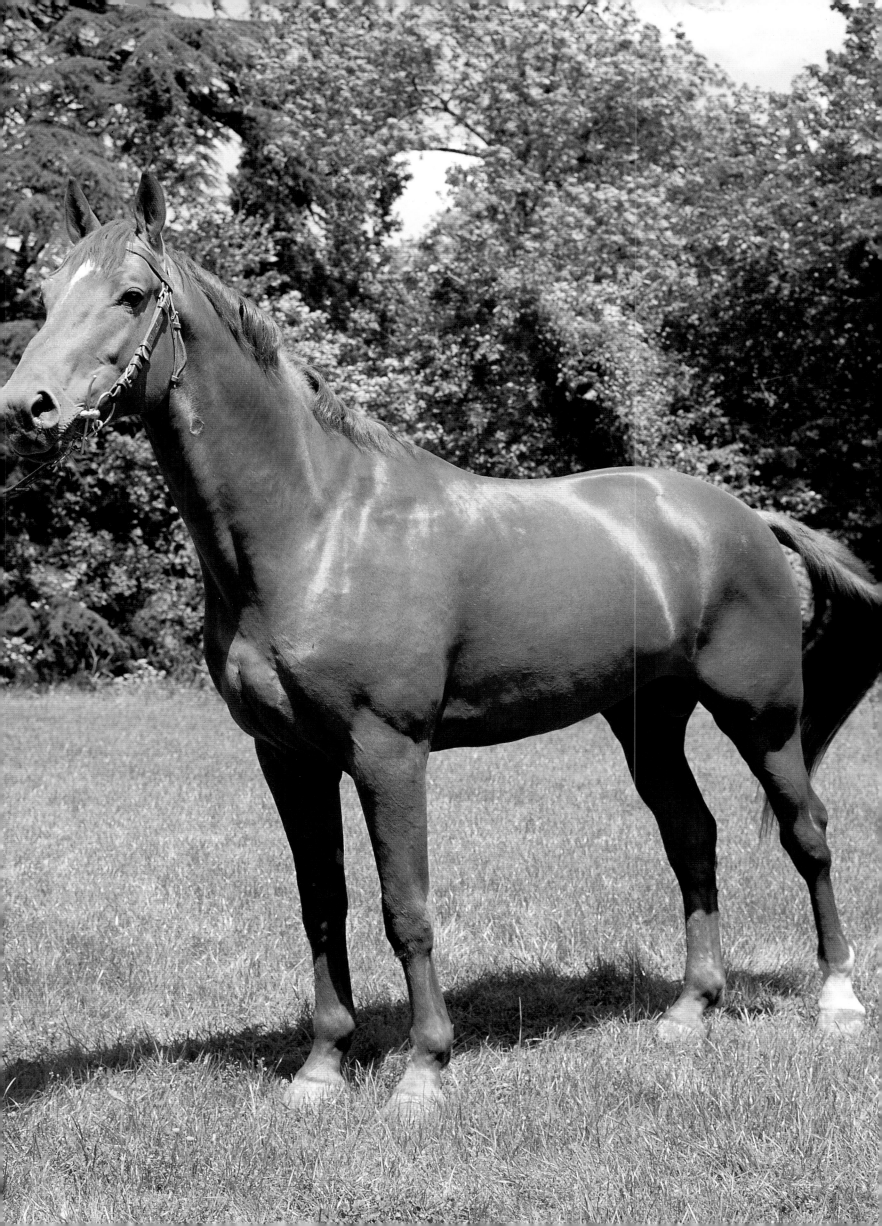

The French Trotter

The origin of French Trotters goes back to the time of horse-drawn carriages. Bred mainly in Lower Normandy, they used to be known as carriage horses. As early as 1830, breeders in this region cross-bred their local horses with a number of Thoroughbred and English horses to improve their stock, especially in terms of physical performance. Cross-breeding and re-crossing in this way made it possible to have horses that were both strong and robust and capable of trotting very fast over many kilometers. From 1850 on, French Trotters were crossed with many other types of horses, such as Norfolks, American Trotters and Russian Orlovs. Like the Anglo-Arab, the Eastern stallion Massoud was one of the founding sires of the breed. Other noteworthy sires are the Thoroughbred The Heir of Linne, the half-bred Young Rattler, and Fuchsia, famous for his black coat, who was the ancestor of more than two thirds of French Trotters. The first harness races were held in 1836 on the beaches at Cherbourg.

Unlike the United States where amblers are used for trotting races, French racing clubs do not race horses with irregular gaits. One of the specialities of France is its *monté* races, i.e. trotting races ridden under saddle. In harness races and trotting races ridden under saddle, the Trotter must at no time break into a gallop, or he will be moved to the outside. The technique consists of having the horse extend the trot to keep him from galloping. Some artificial aids are used to accomplish this: for example, special harnesses that force the horse to keep his head held high, and attaching metal weights to the hooves to extend his stride and make him stay low to the ground.

Generation after generation of Trotters have been selected for their trotting ability. This behavior has gradually become genetically ingrained in the breed, but it is also the product of long and patient training. When breaking a horse in, it is important to stress this gait, so that it becomes systematic, and most of all, regular. Then the young trotter must get used to pulling a large cart called a training rig until he is finally harnessed to a sulky. Now the real training can begin.

A stallion from the Compiègne Stud Farm

Because of the newness of the breed and its extremely diverse ancestry, no real standard model has yet been established. The French Trotter stud book was only begun as recently as 1922, when all Anglo-Normans able to prove their ability to run a kilometer in 1 minute 42 seconds could be registered. In 1941 the stud book was closed, and from then on only horses descending from those already registered qualified for admission. The French Trotter usually has a rather rectilinear profile, a long neck, and a broad chest with well-sprung ribs that enables him to pull a sulky at very high speeds. Height varies from 16.2 to 16.3 hands.

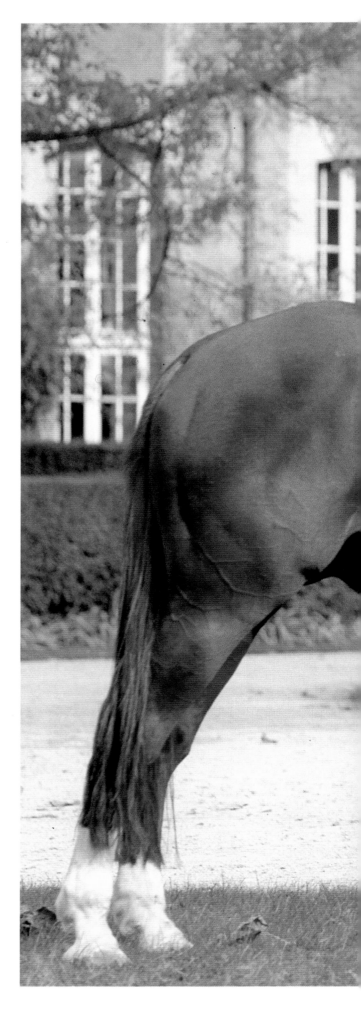

The Camargue

A herd of horses

The conformation of the Camargue (up to 14.2 hands high and 882 lbs.) is reminiscent of horses depicted in prehistoric frescoes. The Camargue must have followed the sea as it receded during the Quaternary Period. Attempts at cross-breeding with Arabians or Barbs have failed, due to the harsh living conditions in the Camargue region where often nothing grows but bindweed and reeds. Because of its ability to survive these tough conditions, the Camargue's strong physical characteristics have always proved dominant. This horse reproduces in the wild. Foals have dark coats which turn gray after their first molt and nearly white around five to seven years of age, when they reach maturity. The local "gardians" (or cowboys) have their own specific lingo for their horses at every age: a foal is a "court", a two year old a "doublen", a three year old a "ternen", a four year old a "quatren", and from the age of five a Camargue horse is a "cavalo". As in every herd, a social hierarchy is established, usually after much battling among stallions. These horses live in a nearly wild habitat where they are free to roam more than two thousand hectares practically untouched by man. They are herded together in groups of about fifty horses, called "manades". Two year old horses are rounded up by the "gardians" and marked on the thigh with their owner's brand. During this period there are many festivals; so too during the "escoussade" (when cattle's ears are cropped) and the "musarlades" (when calves are muzzled), etc. Many equestrian games are held for holidays in Provence and Languedoc. During the festival of Saintes-Maries-de-la-Mer, there are beautiful processions by the sea; the "gardians" proudly don their traditional costumes and straddle their horses, carrying their trident-tipped staffs with banners flying in the wind.

For centuries, these delightful little Camargues have made their home at the embouchure of the Rhône river, among the pink flamingos, the reeds, the sand dunes and the marshes. Galloping so fast through the vast expanses of marsh, splashing and making the water bubble and boil, they are a living symbol of freedom. Their legendary hardiness, equable temperament and endurance have enabled them to adapt to this hostile environment where they are often confronted with wild herds of fierce black bulls.

Many people have been introduced to these unusual horses through the epic poem by Frédéric Mistral *Mirielle* and the famous *Crin Blanc*. Camargues are docile and hardy, with their light gray coats and thick manes. They are highly prized by the *gardians* and are the only horses they will ride. These excellent horsemen are in fact modern day European cowboys who spend their time riding through the marshlands keeping watch over their herds of black cattle, repairing broken fences, selecting bulls and marking their young bull-calves or *anoubles*, with a red-hot brand.

During the winter, when there is less activity, they break in and train the young horses. According to the horsemen, this training can be gentle and gradual, but at times it can also be rather brutal. The Camargue is the sole means of transportation through the *sansouires*, these marshy lands where any vehicle immediately gets stuck in the mud.

When summer comes, the young horses ridden by their *gardians* learn how to round up cattle and lead them into the corral where they can be sorted and isolated. Using the long trident-tipped staff which is the symbol of the Camargue region, the *gardians* separate the animal and lead it toward the pen. The maneuver is often very difficult and dangerous because a young bull will sometimes unexpectedly turn on the horseman, so the horses must be particularly fast and easy to handle.

The bulls are first penned in, then generally trucked to the location of the event in which they are participating. Nevertheless, in order to keep their

traditions alive, the *gardians* sometimes hold an *obrigado*: they encircle the bulls with their horses and lead them into the city, careful not to let any of the animals escape. At the outskirts of the city the villagers take malicious pleasure in trying to frighten the horses, to break up the herd, and free the animals.

The *gardians* thus prove their mastery and skill in capturing the animals who try to run away. During the *abrivado* or period when cattle are being selected it is astonishing to see how an experienced horse not only takes it upon himself to round up the animals, but also how he is able to anticipate their next move.

The Camargue breed was only recognized quite recently, in 1978. The efficiency of the *cavalo* as a herder and the widespread development of equestrian tourism will ensure the future of this marvelous horse whose hardy yet mild temperament make it an ideal mount.

Iberian Horses

The two famous breeds of Portuguese horses are the Lusitano and the Alter-Real. Along with the Andalusian, they embody the pride, elegance and strength of character of horses of the Iberian Peninsula.

With its elevated action, the Lusitano is used as a saddle horse and a light draft horse, and was also formerly used for doing light farm work as well. The origins of the Lusitano's ancestry remain rather vague, but it is quite similar to the Andalusian. In Portugal Lusitanos often participate in bullfights: the mounted *rejoneador* challenges the bull and makes a number of passes, taking great care that his horse does not suffer the slightest scratch. These horses are able to master their fear and flight instinct and are extremely brave.

The Alter-Real is greatly esteemed for dressage exercises and in the Haute Ecole, or High School. It has particularly supple, high, and harmonious action. The Alter-Real is a direct descendent of the three hundred mares that were imported by the House of Bragance to found a stud farm in Vila Portel. It is a horse that is very often used in the equestrian academy of the famous Haute Ecole riding master Nuno de Oliveira, who passed away not too long ago.

There is also the Andalusian which was long associated with Spanish Catholicism. Carthusian monasteries in Jerez, Sevilla and Cazallo first bred Andalusians and they are responsible for preserving the breed. Andalusians derive from stallions imported during the Moorish invasion of the country.

An Andalusian

The Andalusian usually has a gray speckled coat and a very fine, noble head. Over many centuries monks managed to preserve this breed in its original purity. It is an excellent, slow-gaited saddle horse and is the pride of all Spanish horsemen. The Andalusian is also a remarkable circus horse, as it is not only easily trained but also has a proud, harmonious presence. Andalusian blood has influenced many breeds throughout the world, notably the Austrian Lipizzaner, the Russian Orlov, and of course many American horses, as it was Christopher Columbus who repopulated North America with horses.

Italian Horses

Italy was only unified relatively recently, which explains the large number of local breeds. Originating in the Murge region, the Murgese is bred mainly in Abruzzo, Puglia, Basilicata and Calabria. Murgese bloodlines are influenced by cross-breeding with Berber and Arabian stallions during the period of Spanish domination. They are bred practically in the wild in fallow pastures or near forests.

The favorite horse of Italian cowboys, the Maremmana is bred in Latium and Tuscany. It is also used for minor field work. Recently the stock has been improved and refined by the addition of Thoroughbred blood.

The Salernitano, Calabrese, Siciliano and Sanfratellano are light horses which are valued for their sturdiness and docility. The rather large Salernitano horse is often a winner in equestrian competitions. The stock was significantly upgraded at the beginning of the twentieth century through crossing with Thoroughbreds. The other three breeds are used for leisure riding. All the Italian breeds have been influenced by Andalusian, eastern and Thoroughbred horses.

The Lipizzaner

Like the Andalusian, the Lipizzaner is a magnificent horse. A vestige of the ancient Austro-Hungarian empire, it still stands as a symbol of its prestigious past. Its elegance and remarkable abilities in the Haute Ecole make it an excellent parade horse. For more than two hundred years it has been the exclusive mount of the world famous Spanish Riding School of Vienna, which presents superb carousels in its sumptuous baroque ring. Led by riding masters in flamboyant uniforms, the Lipizzaners execute the simplest as well as the most complex figures with unsurpassable grace and harmony. Their high action, which comes from their Andalusian stock, gave rise to a particularly graceful Haute Ecole figure known as the *pas espagnol*.

The breed comes from Lipica, on the present-day Slovenian-Italian border. Lipizzaners used to belong to the Austro-Hungarian empire. The Archduke Charles I had two illustrious Andalusians imported from Spain, the gray-coated Maestoso, and the red roan Favory, who are the forerunners of the breed today. Two Neapolitan horses, Conversano and Napolitain were brought over as well. The mares were mostly imported from Italy. The Lipizzaner's coat is essentially gray. Like all gray coats, the Lipizzaner is foaled with a dark coat which gets lighter very quickly after the first molting.

German and Friesian Horses

Like Italy, until quite recently Germany was divided into numerous dukedoms, kingdoms and other territories. As a result there is a great deal of diversity in horse breeds and types. Most have preserved a trace of their Thoroughbred and Arabian as well as Neapolitan and Spanish (i.e. Andalusian), forerunners. The Oldenburg, Trakehner, Hanoverian and Holsteiner are renowned the world over.

Once a harness horse, over the last decades the Oldenburg has been bred with equestrian competitions in mind. It is a descendant of the Dutch Friesian breed, and used to be a rather heavy work horse. In order to adapt to its present-day application, German breeders have succeeded remarkably well in making the Oldenburg lighter through cross-breeding with Andalusians, Neapolitans, Anglo-Arabs, and Thoroughbreds. It is now an excellent jumper but remains greatly appreciated for its docile temperament.

The Trakehner was formerly used as a cavalry horse for military maneuvers. Frederick I of Prussia founded the breed at the Trakehnen stud farm in 1732. Its great speed made it the best cavalry mount in the 19th century. When the Trakehnen stud farm was nationalized in 1787, there were a dozen studs which foaled more than a thousand horses each. The origins of the Trakehner are complex, but like many breeds, certain traits can be traced back to cross-breeding with Pure-breds.

The Hanoverian is by far the most common horse in Germany. Like many German breeds, it is also the product of cross-breeding between indigenous mares and eastern, Andalusian and Neapolitan sires. The Court of Hanover heartily encouraged breeding Hanoverians. The breed can also be traced back to fourteen black founding Holsteiner sires. In 1714, as the Hanoverian kingdom's ties with England became stronger, cross-breeding with Thoroughbreds increased. The breed was therefore becoming lighter, but this trend was stopped for a time to ensure that the Hanoverian remained essentially a carriage horse. As draft animals began to fall out of use for farm work and horse races, the breed had to become lighter once again. Because of the attributes it has inherited from its past as a harness horse, the Hanoverian is greatly valued for eventing, fox hunting, show-jumping and dressage. Like the Andalusian horse, the Holsteiner was bred in monasteries. The introduction of blood from Thoroughbreds and Yorkshire sires also improved the breed. In recent years the Holsteiner has become wonderfully refined, and has become a marvelous show-jumping horse which can be found in many competitions.

British Horses

Great Britain is of course the realm and the birthplace of the English Thoroughbred. In addition, the British have also developed several other excellent quality Half-breds, such as the Hackney, the Hunter and Welsh Cob.

The Hackney, or English Trotter, is a saddle horse used for leisure harness driving and parade. The Hackney's trot has a high action and is particularly brilliant and elegant. When it trots its forelegs are nearly horizontal. This breed is the product of cross-breeding between Norfolk mares and Yorkshire and Arabian stallions. It is a distinguished horse with proud bearing which has been instrumental in founding other breeds like the Standardbred (American Trotter) and the French Trotter.

The Hunter is particularly well-suited for the hunt with a pack of hounds. It is also successfully used for show-jumping and eventing. It is the product of crosses between Thoroughbred stallions and local indigenous mares. Like the Selle Français, its ancestry is quite varied. It is a horse with great endurance which can bear the weight of a rider for many hours on end, even at high speeds.

The Welsh Cob was once the Welsh peasant's indispensable companion. Cross-breeding between draft horses and Welsh Ponies have given the Welsh Cob its sturdy, strong, if somewhat heavy, conformation. It is particularly robust with great endurance, and is also used as a harness horse and for the hunt. It is very comfortable thanks its stature and can bear quite a heavy-set rider.

A Friesian from the Lucien Gruss Circus

As its name suggests, the Friesian horse originated in Friesland, one of the northernmost provinces of the Netherlands. It is a large, thick-set horse which was once used for heavy cartage. Its conformation has been somewhat refined over the centuries, and has been adapted for pulling lighter and more elegant horse-drawn carriages. Its nobility, dignified bearing, and dark coat make it a favorite harness horse for leisure riding and competitions.

Horses of the East

There are more than forty races of horse to be found in the former Soviet Union, and some have won acclaim world-wide. The Akhal-Teke has been in existence since the dawn of time, and like the Arabian, is a fine desert runner. Originally from Turkmenistan, it is known for its strength and strong will. The Akhal-Teke is an extraordinary performer in endurance and long-distance trials. In 1935, during the 2580 mile "raid" from Ashkhabad to Moscow, one Akhal-Teke managed to cover the entire distance in three days, crossing the 224 miles separating the Kara Kum desert from Moscow without a drop of water. It is also an excellent jumper, and dressage horse (Olympic gold medallist, Rome, 1960). The Turkomans fed their horses pellets of barley and alfalfa wrapped in mutton fat. The Cossacks were responsible for making the Don horse famous. During the First World War, they were still able to assemble more than 132 cavalry regiments and 130,000 cavalrymen who were famous for their great bravery. To frighten and foil the enemy and protect themselves from their fire, the Cossacks would charge at a full gallop, performing spectacular acrobatic military feats called *djighite*. The Don is very hardy and lives in the harsh conditions of the steppes. In the winter the Don will break through the snow to find a few blades of grass to nibble. The influence of Turkmen and Karabakh blood is apparent in its conformation.

The Orlov Trotter is a very finely bred horse, with its nearly white coat. It can be seen harnessed to a magnificent troika, crossing the endless frozen steppes through a snowy haze. The Orlov Trotter is an excellent race horse and the pride of Russian racing buffs. Count Alexei Orlov founded this superb breed in the 1770's at the Khrenov stud farm. He first crossed the Arabian stallion Polkan I with a beautiful Dutch mare. The purity of the Arab-Dutch line was preserved for a long time. Later however, offspring were mated with one another, which, although it contributes to refining the breed, also runs the risks associated with in-breeding. At the foot of the Urals lives the Bashkir horse. Bashkirs are abundant dairy-horses whose milk is used for making kumiss, a low-calorie alcoholic drink.

A Hungarian herd

The vast grassy plains or stuppas which spread out into infinity in Hungary are certainly a paradise for both horses and riders. Four breeds can be found here, the Nonius being the most well-known. The name comes from the Anglo-Norman stallion Nonius I, founding sire of the line in 1810. Hungarian horsemen captured him during the Napoleanic Wars and brought him to the Mezohegyes stud farm. He sired fifteen extremely brilliant stallions out of Arabian, Holsteiner, Lipizzaner, Spanish and Turkish mares. The Nonius is a particularly sturdy horse which is excellent in show-jumping and dressage. Some farmers still use the Nonius as a light draft horse and for working the fields. Most horses of the Russian Empire were the descendants of horses bred and used by primitive pastoral peoples of Central Asia. Przewalski's Horse, or the Asian Wild Horse, which is close to prehistoric horses, can be found on the steppes of Siberia.

American Horses

For some as yet unknown reason the horse population of the Americas disappeared entirely four or five thousand years ago. The species was reintroduced by Christopher Columbus and the first conquistadors, which explains the enormous influence of Spanish blood on all breeds in North and South America. From the beginning of Spanish colonization, Spanish and Portuguese horses, including many mixed-blood Andalusians, became part of the American landscape. For a long time the horse was the sole means of transportation and draft around the farm for immigrants who, in the spirit of the famous voyage of the Mayflower and the gold-rush, were always searching for new lands to conquer.

The Indians of North America captured Mustangs and managed to break them, thereby once again becoming tribes of horsemen. Mustangs are among the horses which returned to the wild in the immensity of the American wilderness which was a perfect habitat for herds of animals to live and roam in freedom.

Cowboys often rode Quarter Horses, which are famous for being able to "stop on a dime" and spin around quickly. Quarter Horses are remarkable for their ability to round up and herd bulls and cattle. The various exercises used by cowboys and their horses can be seen in modern-day rodeo. The cowboy rides into the middle of a ring and must separate a bull-calf from the other animals as quickly as possible without dismounting.

The Quarter Horse no doubt originally comes from Virginia or the Carolinas. In order to intimidate their enemies, the settlers would race their horses down the streets in towns. The speed of the Quarter Horse and its ability to sprint astonishingly fast from a standing start make it an excellent racehorse, as can be witnessed on racecourses all over the United States. Western riding, in which the horse is led with one hand and the rider makes the horse spin around or come to an abrupt stop, or rollback, has become very popular in Europe as well, especially in Germany. Western riding competitions are no longer so unusual in Europe.

The cowboys and settlers also used Morgan horses, descendants of the original unknown sire who in 1790 was given to the inn-keeper Justin Morgan as payment. This little horse was passed along to a number of owners and used for the humblest chores before anyone noticed his exceptional stamina and qualities as a stud horse; he also won many trotting races. All the horses he sired had very dark coats, great endurance and incredible speed, and he was instrumental in founding the Standardbred and American Trotter breeds.

The Appaloosa was the favorite horse of the Nez Percés Indians. They were marvelous horse breeders and succeeded in creating this breed. The Appaloosa's unusual coat is gray with dark speckles. This horse comes from Oregon, near the Palouse River, after which it is named. The Nez Percés were wiped out during the 1870's, at which point the settlers took the Appaloosa and began to standardize its characteristics. The Appaloosa's unusual spotted coat and jocular temperament make it a greatly prized circus horse.

The Pinto has a coat with large splashes of different colors juxtaposing one another. Like the Appaloosa, it is a descendant of the conquistadors' horses which returned to the wild and were subsequently captured by Native Americans. The Indians were fond of these horses with their multi-colored coats. Like all the types of horses which have gone back to the wild, Pintos are marvelous little horses which are very supple and have great endurance.

The origin of the name Palomino comes from the right-hand man of the explorer Cortés, whose name was Don Juan de Palomino. The Palomino's coat is beige to golden, with a flaxen mane. The ancestors of this breed are completely unknown. There remains, however, considerable influence from Arabians. It is an exceptionally pure horse which adapts easily to harsh living conditions and has been the pride of cowboys for generations, for its willing temperament and noble appearance.

A Palomino

Characteristic of this breed is its golden mane. These New World horses have a sprightly look that in spite of everything still conjures up the classic Western in which horse and rider are inseparable companions.

French Draft Horses

Once used for various types of agricultural work, as well as for hauling stagecoaches and heavy horse-drawn drays, the draft horse has been invaluable in human development. Today the draft horse is one of the greatest victims of the industrialization that has taken place in both farming and transportation.

This enormous animal of Herculean strength with its gentle, generous character is gradually disappearing from the French rural landscape. With its legendary easy-going nature and willingness to work hard, the draft horse was the devoted companion not only of generations of farmers, but also of miners, fishermen, movers and bargemen. The inhabitants of the small village of Mollèges in the South of France have erected a monumental sculpture that pays homage to the draft horse and bears witness to its vital importance.

Before the First World War, there were still several million draft horses in France. Today there are only a few thousand remaining and many are bred for their meat. The massive importation of Eastern European horses has caused many breeders to close down. This type of mass breeding does tremendous harm; since only the heaviest types of horses are presently sought after, the great variety of different breeds of draft horses is diminishing and will eventually be radically reduced. In France, several generations of in-breeding the heaviest types of horses among themselves has led to producing animals which are so gargantuan that they are incapable of doing any work at all.

The fast draft horses, known as postiers or post-horses that one used to be able to see speeding down the road drawing stagecoaches, have become very rare in Western Europe. Nevertheless, there are still a few staunch enthusiasts who continue to breed them for horselovers nostalgic for the time of draft animals and the horse-drawn carriage.

Today the trend has come back to refining the breeds somewhat to encourage pleasure harness driving and trekking. Green tourism has popularised weekend excursions for city-dwellers in which they discover the countryside in every detail, and are

A Boulonnais

Native of the North of France, the Boulonnais is the horse most threatened by extinction. There are also risks due to in-breeding, as the Boulonnais population dwindles and the gene pool is reduced. As a result of having been cross-bred with Arabians in former days, this splendid horse has an exceptionally noble temperament and a very refined, elegant appearance, with his head held proud and high. His coat is essentially gray, sometimes dappled. Like all draft horses, these heavy horses were used for heavy farm labor. However, in France the wholesale fish merchants, or "mareyeurs", used a faster, lighter type that came to be known as a Mareyeur. They would deliver fish in Paris in the small horse-drawn carts filled with ice called "Ballons de marée". The breed suffered tremendous losses in the bombings during the Second World War and under German occupation.

swayed by the gentle rhythm of the horse's gait and the clopping of his hooves. In some forests the draft horse is being put back to work for unlading, i.e. clearing the forest of felled wood and hauling the logs to the roadside where they are loaded onto trucks.

This utilization of the draft horse has many economic, ecological and practical advantages. It makes it possible to fell only those trees which must be removed and not an entire swathe of trees to clear a path big enough for a motor vehicle to pass through.

Unlike tractors and gigantic bulldozers, draft horses can weave their way through the small spaces between the trees with great precision. They work tirelessly without causing damage to trees as they pass and without destroying the ground by creating ruts, uprooting clumps of earth, or making vibrations that are harmful to the environment. The draft horse is often the only viable solution for the upkeep and responsible development of mountainous or very rough woodland areas. For all these reasons this type of heavy work horse is making a certain comeback in mountain forests in Germany, Belgium and France (e.g. in the Jura, Ardennes, and Morvan).

As small scale farms are gradually disappearing, there are more and more fallow fields which must be attended to in order to avoid the risks of fire and avalanches in mountainous regions. Some breeders put their draft horses out to pasture to keep the grasses and underbrush in the fields well-trimmed. Others use them to mow the high grasses before the onset of winter on steeply inclined slopes. Some rural people use draft horses for pleasure but also because they are capable of plowing with such great precision. Unfortunately, however convincing these arguments may be, they are not enough to revive breeding of these magnificent, powerfully broad-chested, even-tempered, lovable horses.

Horse pulls and surrogate mothers

The Haras Nationaux is working along with other organizations to try and come up with possibilities for the future of this warm-hearted animal. Experiments using brood-mares as surrogate mothers have been attempted, for example. The fetuses of mares who compete at the highest level have been successfully transplanted. This process considerably shortens the gestation and immobilization period of a competition mare, which is, of course, advantageous to her career.

The renewed interest in regional folklore and old-fashioned country celebrations, e.g. sowing, harvesting, and threshing festivals, is also helping pull the draft horse out of the shadows. Horse pulls and log-hauling and plowing contests attract very enthusiastic audiences. Draft horse pulling is an equestrian sport that comes from Japan in which draft horses on a grass track are harnessed to heavy, cast iron sleighs. The contestants must pull their loads uphill over a slope of built up earth situated in front of them on the track.

An Ardennais

Probably the descendant of prehistoric horses from Solutré (50,000 BC), the Ardennais developed into three different types of horses: in France the Ardennais of the North, by far the most massive and impressive of all, and in Belgium, the Belgian Draft horse and the Brabant. These enormous horses of common ancestry enjoy the largest geographic area in Western Europe. They used to be put to work cultivating the beet and potato fields as well as clearing logs from the forest. They were also used for pulling heavy carts full of coal in the mines. Once they had gone down into the mines and underground tunnels, some never saw the light of day again. Particularly tough and powerful, they were also used in the artillery for firing and moving canons. These horses also distinguished themselves for their impressive endurance and stamina during the disastrous retreat of the Napoleonic army from Moscow.

French breeds

France has nine great draft horse breeds: the Ardennais, Auxois, Boulonnais, Breton, Cob, Comtois, Percheron, Trait du Nord, and Poitevin (a breed of mule) as well as the Poitou Ass.

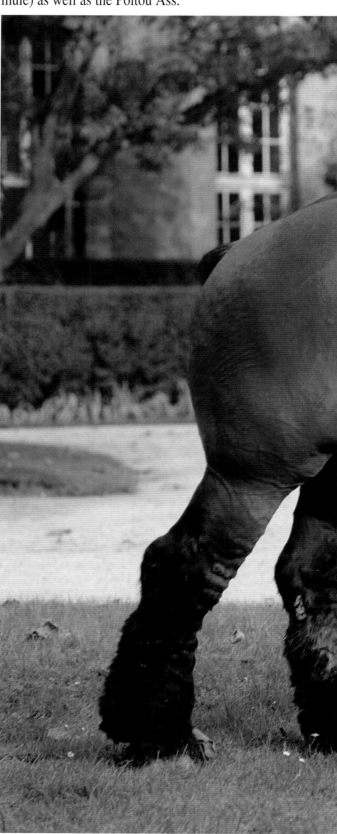

These breeds have evolved over the ages. Like the Boulonnais, there are two different types of Breton horse: one is a heavier horse that was used for working the fields and pulling stagecoaches, and the other lighter type which was used for pulling postal vehicles, whence the name Postier Breton (Brittany post horse). This fast, supple horse, known as the Ronsin, was the mount of Celtic warriors; it was used in the Middle Ages as a combat horse by knights wearing heavy armor.

The Crusaders and the Templars were fond of the Breton Draft horse, which has been strongly influenced by Arabian stock. These horses were often subsequently cross-bred with Norfolk Roadsters as well.

Whole regions owed their livelihood to the work of these horses and they participated in the Procession of Pardons. In the ports they helped unload the fishing boats and transport merchandise.

The Auxois, whose conformation is quite close of that of the Ardennais, is dangerously close to

extinction. Research has shown that there are now fewer than three hundred breed mares extant. This heavily built, powerful horse from Burgundy, weighing in at about 1654 lbs. to 1 ton, was once used for drawing heavy chariots and carriages. Being a horse from the Burgundy region, the Auxois also worked weeding the vineyards, pulling enormous tipcarts of grapes at harvest time, and delivering the heavy barrels of wine piled high on gigantic carriages all over France.

The Comtois is a broad-backed draft horse with a coat that is sometimes roan, sometimes bay, and a magnificent golden mane. The Comtois was the favorite mount of the Burgundian knights, from the northernmost point of ancient Germania, who invaded Gaul in the 3rd century. From this period on, the Comtois was bred in the Franche-Comté and in the Jura regions of France. Having evolved in very mountainous terrain, this horse has a highly-developed sense of balance which enables it to climb up and down extremely steep inclines, but also very narrow winding paths with vertiginous drop-offs. A large Comtois fair takes place every year in Maîche in the Doubs, not far from the Swiss border. More than three hundred horses are presented for the gait class show. This is usually where the Haras Nationaux buys new Comtois studs to re-stock their various stud farms. During the gathering there are many traditional demonstrations, shows and competitions, such as bareback stallion riding races, and harness races in which brood mares pull flat wagons.

The Norman Cob is a particularly light variety of draft horse once used for driving hackneys and other one-person carriages because of its supple, fast pace. They were often to be found on the market place hauling tip-carts and wagons full of farm-fresh vegetables. Like its British namesake, the Welsh Cob, the Norman Cob is not a standardized, precisely defined breed. It is a type of horse, in between a saddle horse and a draft horse which can easily fulfill both functions. It is an extraordinarily docile and elegant horse, as one can see at the stud farms at de Pin, Angers, and most of all, Saint-Lô, where the Norman Cob is king. At Saint-Lô, these horses are often harnessed for pleasure or parade. Both their temperament and conformation hint at the influence of the Breton Draft Horse and Percheron bloodlines.

A Percheron

The Percheron is the most common draft horse, both in France and abroad. It was once used as a carriage horse and for urban transportation. In the 1900's, magnificent teams of six to eight horses used to draw huge double-decker omnibuses as big as train cars along the grand Parisian thoroughfares. The Percheron was also an extraordinarily energetic work horse used around the farm and for plowing the fields. The most common coat is dappled gray, but they also come in roan and black. There are a number of Percheron breeders in the United States, where they have been imported on a large scale. Harness-driving enthusiasts still have them draw superb delivery wagons. Percherons are commonly seen in Japan where they compete in the very popular draft horse-pull competitions. Every four years the Percheron breeding unions hold a huge meeting in a different country, and bring together breeders from all over the world. These encounters are enlivened by events such as demonstrations, gait class shows, and harnessing and plowing competitions.

The British Draft Horse

In Great Britain draft horses are particularly beautiful. In a kingdom which has kept many of its traditions alive, Shires have the privilege of drawing the sumptuous carriages which convey the royal family during special state occasions. Their coats gleaming, in their finest shining harnesses and silver tack, they parade from Buckingham Palace to Saint Paul's Cathedral where royal ceremonies are celebrated. Besides the Percheron, which is of French origin, there are four prestigious breeds to be found here: the Shire, the Clydesdale, the Suffolk and the Cleveland Bay. However, as eating horsemeat is forbidden in Great Britain, breeding these horses is becoming increasingly rare.

The Shire has come down to us from antiquity. Impressed by the horse's sheer enormity (often as tall as 17.2 hands high and weighing more than one and a half tons), the Romans dubbed him Equus Magnus. Until the Middle Ages Shires were essentially used for combat, both in the cavalry and for knights in armor.

The Clydesdale is another draft horse that is as powerful as it is elegant. The breed originated in Scotland. Although less massive and of lighter build, its conformation is close to that of the Shire, and the Clydesdale is sometimes referred to as the Scottish Shire. It gets its name from the river Clyde which runs through the county of Lanarkshire. Clydesdales were used more as pack horses for transporting merchandise than for draft. During the industrial revolution breeders began raising more powerful draft horses to be used for supplementary power and transport. Like the Shire, the Clydesdale was used in the mines, for conveying travelers and in distilleries where large whisky barrels had to be moved around. These horses were exported and were responsible for the creation of a number of stud farms in the United States as well as exerting a strong influence on Eastern European draft horse breeds.

Suffolks, which are extremely corpulent, are known for their longevity, and sometimes live to be more than twenty years old. Suffolks come from East Anglia, and unfortunately, are threatened with extinction. In spite of the particular attention being paid to this breed, only a few hundred remain today. According to certain specialists they are one of the purest breeds of draft horses. From their ascendant, the stallion Crisp's Horse of Ufford, Suffolks have inherited their chestnut coat and beautiful sandy manes.

A Shire

The colossal power of the Shire makes him excel at the extremely arduous task of timber-hauling. Shires unladed tree-trunks, delivered gigantic barrels of beer, and pulled wagons in the mines. Their hauling power can be as much as fifty tons from a standstill. The Shire's coat is usually black bay or more rarely, gray. His lower legs are covered with large tufts of white hair which are so fine and silky they are called feathers.

The Cleveland Bay, with its unusual black-specked bay coat, comes from Yorkshire in Northern England. It is one of the oldest British breeds, and is highly prized for its strong constitution and large size, which it transmits to offspring when crossed with other breeds.

Cross-breeding with Thoroughbreds and Arabians has created the excellent horses known as Hunters. As it was the tireless travelling companion of peddlers and wool and crockery salesmen, people referred to the Cleveland Bay as "Chapman", or notions dealer.

BREEDING

Reproduction

Thanks to the role played by the Haras Nationaux (the national stud farms), horse breeding in France is now done increasingly rationally. At one time it used to lack sufficient stock, and horses had to be imported to re-stock the different cavalry regiments. Nowadays this no longer holds true, and in addition to large scale production, France has earned a solid reputation for its high quality.

For a long time the rich pastures of Normandy were the main horse-breeding region. Today this region still boasts the greatest number of stud farms in France, but they can also be found all over the country. Although the breeding of draft horses is in sharp decline due to mechanization in rural areas, the growing interest in equitation has done wonders for breeding sport and leisure horses.

Selection of the stallion

Before having his or her mare covered, the breeder painstakingly selects the stallion to be used as stud based on criteria which include his origins, his athletic performance and that of his descendants. There are two possibilities open to the breeder: either to call upon the services of the Haras Nationaux, which has at its disposal top quality stallions in every district in France, or to go to a private stud farm where the price for having a mare covered is often higher, but there are other prestigious sires available.

The first sexual instincts in a colt or a filly seem to be just more frolicking and playing. Instinctively, while continuing to enjoy themselves and bite one another playfully, they will sometimes get into very characteristic, suggestive positions. The males start to be sexually active as yearlings. It is therefore important at this age to either castrate them or separate them from the fillies and mares.

A highly developed maternal instinct

The young foal never wanders far from his mother. He spends most of his time playing alone, resting in the grass and nursing. When he strays a bit too far away, his mother whinnies and he immediately comes back.

Good stud stallions can cover four or five mares in one day, if they are in good health and fed a high energy diet.

When a mare is in heat and fertile, she makes her condition known by urinating; her urine has a specific odor during these periods. Usually, instead of violently rejecting the stallion, she herself becomes very insistent. The male knows from her smell that he can approach her without fear. He often reacts to her enticement by curling back his upper lip in a gesture known as flehmen. In the wild, as well as under the watchful eye of the breeder, penetration is rather brief and sometimes quite brutal.

As the mare approaches, the horse neighs and stamps the ground, then rears up and comes down onto the mare's back to begin mating. A mare is usually in heat every twenty-one to twenty-five days, which corresponds to her periods of fertility. She is rarely in heat in the wintertime, and these periods are closer together in summer. She will not allow a stallion to come near her unless she is in heat.

Gestation

The gestation period usually lasts eleven months. Breeders generally calculate when they will have their mares covered so that foaling can take place in summertime. Two weeks after being fertilized, the fetus can be seen in an ultrasound scan. From the sixth or seventh month on the foal takes on more weight inside its mother's belly.

By the ninth month, it will have gained half of its birth-weight. When a mare is gravid, she must be very closely watched in order to avoid accidents or miscarriages. Her feed must also be fortified so that she has enough vitamins, calcium and minerals for the healthy development of her foal.

Foaling

Covering

Often in order to refine or increase the value of his stock, the breeder will try to establish and strengthen bloodlines through cross-breeding certain offspring repeatedly. Care must be taken however not to over-breed the same stock, to avoid the risks involved in in-breeding. Artificial insemination is now lessening this threat by making it possible to transport semen cheaply and easily. Generally a saddle horse becomes a stallion at the age of three, a Thoroughbred at the age of five, and a trotter at around seven.

Foaling, or the birth of the foal, is always a marvelous, magical moment. There are certain tell-tale signs that foaling is imminent, such as swelling of the teats, the appearance of a wax-like substance on the nipples, and the muscles of the croup relaxing. At this point it is wise to lead the mare into a spacious box that is well-lined with clean straw and check on her frequently.

When the mare lies down and her contractions begin, it is important to be as discreet as possible and not to interfere unless it is absolutely necessary.

Foaling should not last more than about forty-five minutes. Normally the foal is born face forward, hooves first, head held close to the forelegs. The amniotic fluid and membrane are then expelled. When the foal is resting on the straw, someone must very quietly check that this membrane has indeed torn open so the foal can breathe. The mother is very attentive to her foal and lies by his side for some time. She then proceeds to lick his still wet coat and take in his odor. They are still attached to one another by the umbilical cord, which will break by itself when the foal moves or the mare stands up. A foal making his first awkward attempts to stand up on his long, gangly limbs is always a very touching sight.

The new-born foal must learn almost immediately how to stand on his own two legs in order to drink his first mother's milk, called colostrum or beestings, which is very rich and contains all the antibodies he will need to strengthen his immune system. He must also quickly expel the thick, dark waste matter in his intestinal track called meconium. Wide-eyed and hesitant on his spindly legs, the new-born foal is ready to follow his mother.

From foal to adult

Until they are a year old colts and fillies are called foals, and then they are known as yearlings.

The mare's milk production keeps increasing for two months and then begins to gradually diminish. Either out of curiosity or for fun, the foal begins to nibble on grass and to play with his feed.

The breeder therefore often makes a special enclosure and leaves barley and grain out just for the foals.

In order to make training easier later, during this period it is important for the young horse to come into frequent contact with people, to get used to having the halter slipped on, and to be willing to give his hoof to the breeder. Then comes the time when colts and fillies start to become more independent and begin frolicking together, biting each other playfully, and leaping and running all over.

Weaning

At the age of six months, the mare begins to have less milk, and she must not be tired out. The time for weaning has come. The foals are separated from their mother, and put in a pasture far enough away from the mare that they cannot see or hear one another. They are grouped together to form another herd, with an old horse or an old mare.

After one or two months, the mares will have forgotten them and will no longer be lactating; the foals can once again be brought back into the original herd. During the weaning process, the mare's teats must be closely watched to make sure they do not become engorged. Once they are one year old, the young males are separated from the rest of the herd. Around eighteen months the decision must be made whether to castrate them or leave them entire. If they are not going to become sires, they will become geldings, which are often more docile and easier to handle.

Feeding the young foal

During the first three months the foal grows very rapidly, so his diet must be extremely rich to give him the strength he needs until his mother begins to produce less milk. During the first weeks his feeds are very close together, then become progressively further apart. The young foal begins to complement his diet -first out of curiosity then out of necessity- by grazing or eating barley, oats, or whatever grains are put in his feed trough.

Following pages
An Arabian broodmare with her foal

One of the particularities of Arabians is that they can adapt to every climate. The damp climate in Normandy, where there are an abundance of stud farms, suits them perfectly.

Breaking in

Training a horse on the lunge

Training sessions take place in the wee hours of the morning so the horse won't be bothered by the sun or the heat. The Gardes Républicains, who run a restocking department of more than 500 horses, break in all their own mounts. They pay particular attention to this phase in the life of a horse, because, like his rider, the horse must be perfectly disciplined all throughout his career.

Breaking in is the first step in training. The horse must learn to withstand the presence and weight of the rider and to respond to the orders he is given. It is a magical period in which an extremely strong bond is forged between man and horse; it is easy to imagine how this phenomenon could have inspired the fabulous ancient myth of the centaur.

The use of good psychology and a gentle hand can thus triumph over the tremendous raw power and energy of the horse. If early on an atmosphere of trust between the young horse and humans has already been established, the task will be significantly easier.

If racehorses begin training at the age of two, at the risk of harming the still growing horses and eventually shortening their careers, leisure and sport horses only begin training at the age of three.

In some places, such as South America, training is sometimes violent and severe. In Europe and the United States however, it is usually done gently and with respect for the animal. Rushing through the various steps can compromise the quality of the training.

Here too, as the moral of the fable *The Lion and the Rat* by Jean de La Fontaine reminds us:

"Patience and biding one's time
Are more effective than force or rage".

Above all, the horse must have learnt to withstand the bit, a mouthpiece with two moveable steel rings which is used to stop and lead him. The horse must also get used to the saddle, which is called "backing a horse". This is done by placing a small padded girth known as a surcingle on his back and strapping it loosely under his belly. In this way he is reassured and more relaxed and will be able perform the exercises he is taught more easily. Regular daily twenty or thirty minute sessions are sufficient.

Lungeing

The very first step is lungeing, which is done on foot without a rider. The horse is tethered to his handler by a long lead known as a lunge rein, which is attached either to the horse's bit or to his cavesson (a sturdy leather halter with a noseband). Then the horse is encouraged to move in circles around his trainer in the three gaits, to stop and change hands, or to swing around and walk in the other direction. It takes several lessons to master these tasks. The voice is the most essential aid for urging the horse on and rewarding him for doing his exercises correctly. It is not unusual for a horse to take fright and have a tendency to rear up during his first session. It is important to remain calm and to take the time to reassure him. While training on the lunge, the horse is made to move forward using the voice, by pulling or releasing the lunge rein, and if necessary, through moderate and judicious use of the chambrière or lungeing whip (a long, rigid-handled whip). Often just the sight of the lungeing whip is enough to set the horse back on track.

As the training progresses, small obstacles are placed in the horse's path that he must step over or jump over. It is also possible to practice using long reins to complete these lessons. Two lunge reins are attached to the outer rings of the horse's bit; the trainer stands just behind and follows along with the horse as he executes the various movements requested. To put the horse at ease and teach him how to jump over obstacles unhampered, this training should be done in a large ring or arena where he can move about freely. The horse will respond to voice aids and the lungeing whip.

Mounting a horse

Before the horse can be mounted it is essential that he has mastered all the phases of training done on the lunge with his trainer on foot. First the horse must get used to wearing a saddle, which must be gently placed on his back and very loosely strapped. Then exercises should be continued on the lunge, without a rider. At first the horse may react violently, bucking and trying to bolt, as in a rodeo. Once again it is essential for the trainer to stay calm and to reassure the horse using his or her voice. To keep him from breaking the lunge rein or tearing up his mouth with the bit from thrashing around, he must at all costs be made to stay on his circular path and go forward. Over the following days when the horse has calmed down, small sandbags can be attached to his saddle to simulate the weight of the rider.

The lesson on mounting is an important one. The handler walks up to the horse's head and talks to him to distract his attention and keep him calm. In the meantime, an assistant approaches the horse from the left, steps into the stirrup and straightens his leg. He repeats this same gesture many times without going any further until the horse does not flinch at all. Later on the assistant will try letting himself be carried by the horse, draping his body over the horse like a sack of potatoes, with his ribcage pressed against the saddle. When the trainer thinks the horse is ready to carry the rider, the assistant positions himself correctly with one foot in each stirrup trying to make himself as light as possible. The horse will continue to circle around the ring on the lunge as before. Gradually he will learn to respond to "aids", directions the rider gives with his calves, as well as the way he or she handles the reins. The way a horse is trained at the early stages conditions his behavior for the rest of his life and determines his career. He must therefore be tactfully trained under the best possible conditions using good psychology. It is for this reason that many breeders and owners have their horses trained by professionals at riding clubs and stables.

The Haras Nationaux

Founded by Colbert in 1665, the French national stud farms, the Haras Nationaux, are the showcase of horse-breeding in France. The main role of this administrative body is to preserve and improve the genetic stock of French horse breeds. Under the aegis of the Ministry of Agriculture, the Haras Nationaux go to great efforts to buy the best stallions and send them to various stud farms all over the country in order to offer breeders the possibility of refining their stock through high quality cross-breeding. For a nominal sum, many sires that are famous for their bloodlines and their athletic performance or that of their descendants are thus made available to breeders. When there is too much demand for a stallion, lots are drawn. Mares with the best genetic ratings (based on their offspring and their results in competitions) are always given top priority. The mares are covered in hand under the guidance of one of the Haras stallion handlers. Artificial insemination is done here as well.

The Haras Nationaux run twenty-three stud farms throughout France. There are also several re-stocking centers in each French department so every region in France is effectively covered. The often magnificent historic buildings which house the Haras Nationaux stud farms also add to their renown.

At the crack of dawn the Haras guards begin cleaning the bedding of the horses which are kept in superb boxes and wooden stalls with plaited straw-covered floors. Saddle horses and draft horses alike are fed, then carefully groomed till their flawless coats shine. The guards then take each stallion out for exercise, and either ride or harness the horse or let it run free. The teams of two, four, six or even eight horses prancing around the Haras courtyard in their gleaming harnesses is a truly marvelous spectacle to behold. They are harnessed to a sparkling berlin and led by a guard in a uniform decorated with silver braid.

Almost all the French horse breeds are represented in each stud farm. How many of each breed are in each location depends on regional breeding patterns and the origins of the different breeds. Consequently, there are more Anglo-Arabs in the Southwest and at the Haras de Pompadour and more Trotters and Thoroughbreds in Brittany and Normandy. Every stud farm is run by a Haras officer who is an Ingénieur des Eaux et des Forêts (Water and Forest Engineer). He is assisted by officers as well as a veterinarian. Besides selecting horses and overseeing their reproduction, the Haras advise breeders on their choice of sires.

A team of five Percherons in front of the Haras du Pin stud farm.

There is no longer any trace of the first royal stud farm (Haras Royal) founded by Colbert in Montfort l'Amaury. Despite its name, it was actually a private stud farm. The Haras du Pin and Haras de Pompadour are among the oldest and most prestigious stud farms in existence. The Haras du Pin is housed in a splendid edifice which dates back to the last years of the reign of Louis XIV (1714). The building is the home of more than seventy-five stallions, and was designed especially for this purpose by the famous architect Mansart. The surrounding terraces and garden lanes are the work of the renowned French garden designer Le Nôtre. In these magnificent quarters the famous Ecole d'élèves d'officiers des Haras trains its administrators. There is also an apprenticeship program where young people between fourteen and sixteen can learn to become farriers or grooms. Every year large equestrian events are held here which include eventing, harness racing, and show-jumping.

In order to encourage quality breeding, they also hold gait class shows in which brood-mares and young horses are judged on their behavior and conformation. But their involvement is even more far-reaching. The Haras Nationaux are also active in certain technical and economic sectors. They finance research on breeding and scientific methods of reproduction such as embryo transfer as well as encouraging development of equestrian sport and leisure activities. They monitor and aid local riding clubs and stables, and act as a regulatory authority for races. The Haras Nationaux take a commission on every bet placed to finance their activities and maintain very close ties with racetracks and riding clubs.

Pompadour

The Château

The Château de la Pompadour, or Pompadour Castle, built as solidly as a fortress, is a far cry from the frivolities of Versailles, but its equestrian tradition harks back to the time of Louis XIV.

This is the undisputed realm of the Anglo-Arab breed. The Haras de Pompadour now occupies this castle that Louis XV once bequeathed to his favorite mistress, the famous Marquise de Pompadour. The Marquise owned this castle but never actually lived in it. It then became the property of the Duke de Choiseul, who in 1761 traded it with the king for the Château d'Amboise. It was at this time that Louis XV decided

upon the building's new vocation. In 1837 it was converted into a racecourse, and every year some of the most highly reputed races in the Southwest of France and many competitions take place there. Less than 100 yards from the castle, the du Puy Marmont stud farm, with its beautiful shady park, houses a number of stallions, mostly Arabians, Thoroughbreds and Anglo-Arabs. Here breeders have at their disposal a highly renowned stock of sires. Just a little over a mile away, right in the center of town, is the brood-mare stable at la Rivière. Studs to cover these state brood-mares are

chosen from among those at de Puy Marmont. The foals are subsequently sold for the upkeep of the grounds, while certain colts are kept for the Haras' re-stocking department, just as some fillies are kept for the brood-mare re-stocking.

The Anglo-Arabs record of achievements in competition is a glorious one. There was the unforgettable *Ali-Baba* ridden by Pierre Jonquères d'Oriola, individual Olympic gold medallist in show-jumping in 1952. Jiva performed magnificently at the Los Angeles Olympics in 1984.

S.I.R.E.: a computerized repertory

Created in 1974 near the Haras National de Pompadour, the S.I.R.E., (System of Identification for the Repertory of Equidae) is in charge of coordinating and managing the registration of horses and ponies and data concerning them throughout France. In 1992 the figures showed 630,000 horses on file, 170,00 draft horses and 90,000 ponies. After having recorded and verified reproduction, the S.I.R.E. publishes papers for every horse at birth. It transmits the identity of horses to clubs which hold races and competitions. The National Institute of Agronomic Research then analyzes the results and calculates the genetic indices which are entered into the public registry file in Pompadour. All S.I.R.E. data is available to the public over the Internet. In this way the activity of every breeder can be oriented as effectively as possible in keeping with his or her specific criteria.

EQUESTRIAN DISCIPLINES

The Cadre Noir de Saumur and the E.N.E.

The Cadre Noir is the product of a long process of evolution. In the 18th century the Ecole de Versailles supplied the army with officers who were more enamoured of riding indoors around the ring than in the field on military campaigns. The cavalry generals were eventually roused to action and created the Ecole des Chevaux Légers de la Garde in Versailles, also constructing the ring for the Ecole Militaire, headed by Jacques d'Auvergne, the founding father of French military equestrianism. It soon became a school and trained, among others, the Regiment des Carabiniers of the Count de Provence when they came to Saumur in 1763. Saumur began to have such a distinguished reputation that all the French regiments sent their commissioned and non-commissioned officers there, and other schools were eventually forced to close their doors. Saumur became the Ecole d'Application de la Cavalerie.

With the onset of the French revolution, Saumur was to have its share of ups and downs. From 1814 on, there were two types of teachers: on the one hand military instructors and on the other civilian horsemen and retired military men whose aim was to create an equestrian academy for the personal betterment of officers. This was the forerunner of the Saumur school which would later become known as the Cadre Noir. It has been run by thirty-four master horsemen thus far, among them some of the world's greatest equestrians, such as General l'Hotte. On May 17 1972, the day after the gala evening when the Cadre Noir performed a traditional series of dressage figures for Queen Elizabeth of England, the Journal Officiel published the Decree of May 16th, in the name of the Ministry of Youth, Sport and Leisure, creating the Ecole Nationale d'Equitation. The Cadre Noir left the Ecole de Cavalerie to join the new institution at this time.

All E.N.E. classes are taught by master horsemen, many of them in the military; education is the school's main focus. Nowadays it is through the Cadre Noir that the Ecole Nationale maintains its influence and promulgates French horsemanship. Parisians had the chance to experience the Cadre Noir's virtuosity first hand in May 1992, when they performed for the public at Bercy, in celebration of the school's twentieth anniversary. Traditional series of dressage figures and exercises and the more elaborate gala performances attract more than 50,000 visitors every year. These events take place at Terrefort near Saumur, where the school has been located since 1984. It is situated on a 300 hectare site with 10 Olympic size arenas, almost 25 miles of tracks, a veterinary clinic, an auditorium and five rings, including that of the Cadre Noir which seats 1,500 spectators.

The purpose of the two traditional series of figures is simply to illustrate the principles of the French School, in which emphasis is placed on the precision of the figures as a group, the uniformity of the paces, bearing, and details of individual execution.

There is a series of outdoor jumping figures which is reminiscent of its Ecole de Versailles heritage. It has preserved three of the elevated airs which were adapted to a 19th century military context: the *Courbette*, the *Croupade*, and the *Cabriole*. The other series, which is performed in an indoor ring, is a reflection of the style of the French School and can truly be called equestrian choreography.

The Ecole Nationale d'Equitation has made it possible to maintain a tradition whose roots are in the military and to reinforce this tradition with the professional technique the equestrian academy demands.

Colonel Carde, Master Equestrian of the Cadre Noir

This horse is galloping in duple time; after the right hindleg touches down he follows with the right diagonal. For 170 years in Saumur outdoor riding has been practiced with as much success as Haute Ecole horsemanship.

Opposite
A Croupade

The Cadre Noir have preserved some of the elevated airs from the classical equestrian arts, which were adapted to the needs of 19th century military instruction.

Left
A Cabriole

"The cabriole is the most elevated and most perfect of all jumps. When the horse is in the air, with hind and forequarters at an equal height, he kicks his legs out so forcefully, it is as if he would separate them from himself, as it were, with his hindlegs darting out behind him like a shot."

La Guérinière
Ecole de Cavalerie, 1731

SAUMUR

Croupade à la main

In this movement the horse goes into a kick from a standstill, his forelegs remaining on the ground. This jump is peculiar to the Saumur school and differs from the Versailles croupade in which the horse "pulls his hindlegs under his belly".

SAUMUR AND VIENNA: TWO HAUTE ECOLE TRADITIONS

SAUMUR

Terre-à-terre

This is a very particular gait, a sort of gallop in duple time which is very collected. The horse moves forward in a succession of small bounds. This is the gait the horse takes in preparation for that most spectacular of Haute Ecole jumps, the cabriole.

VIENNA

The Spanish School of Vienna

The Spanish School of Vienna sets the standard for the most traditional 18th century style classic equestrian art; it was created in the Viennese court and has never strayed far from the original precepts of La Guérinière. The School style is mostly centered around Haute Ecole elevated airs and jumps.

The allusion to Spain in the name comes from the first horses used, which were a Spanish breed, the Andalusian. The Austrians cross-bred these horses with indigenous breeds, and created the superb breed known as the Lipizzaner, which are the only mounts used by the Viennese horsemen. All the horses presented are entire. Their training only begins when they are four years old, and is extremely thorough and gradual. Horses are not ridden until they have been trained on the lunge for two full years. These remarkably noble horses add to the matchless reputation of the school.

With the fall of the Austro-Hungarian Empire the School became a state institution, and only survived thanks to the tireless devotion and considerable fortune of the Count Von der Straten. Threatened once again with extinction as Allied troops were advancing near the end of the Second World War, the School was able to escape ruin by moving into the American zone of occupation.

A purely oral tradition

Performances of the Spanish School of Vienna are given in the splendid baroque style ring located at the corner of Josephsplatz. The traditions and teaching are handed down orally from horseman to horseman. In 1814, all the kings of Europe were invited to a remarkable carousel, but otherwise no public performances were given until 1920.

Its ceremony has remained unchanged since its inception. Ten horsemen present themselves in ceremonial uniform similar to the Saumur uniforms. The Grande Reprise figures from the Haute Ecole are executed in the purest style and come straight out of the grandest equestrian tradition.

Above
School of Vienna jumps

The jumps executed at the School of Vienna adhere strictly to the definitions given in 1778 by Montfaucon de Rogles, the only Versailles horseman who left a written record of his teaching.

Opposite
A Levade

The levade was called a Pesade in Versailles. The horse rears up with the fore-quarters on his completely bent hind legs and pauses, putting all his weight on his hind legs.

The Garde Républicaine

The Garde Républicaine, or Republican Guard, carries on the heritage of all the military corps which, since the first Frankish kings, have assured the protection of Paris, the security of its institutions and the honor of the highest state authorities. From the early Guet Royale to the present-day Garde Républicaine, there have been more than sixty corps which have succeeded one another under various regimes. It was during the 18th century that the Guet began to be called the Garde de Paris, or Paris Guard.

In 1789, the Garde de Paris was disbanded and its members became part of the Garde Nationale. The Decree of 12 Vendémiaire of the Year XI (October 4, 1802), created the Garde Municipale de Paris, made up of 180 cavalrymen and 2550 infantrymen. From 1805 on, the Garde participated in the Napoleonic campaigns. For Napoleon, "A troop charged with maintaining order within the homeland should not be deprived of the honor of serving its grandeur outside. It will only be bettered and more highly respected." Arms were a fact of life during the imperial period. In 1807, in Danzig, the Garde attacked the British warship the "Dauntless" from small boats. In 1808 it took the bridge of Alcoléa, thus opening the route to Cordoba to the French Army. Other armed conflicts in Friedland (1807) and Burgos (1812) would only confirm the Garde Républicaine's character as an elite troop.

In 1813, at the impetus of General Malet, the Garde was disbanded and replaced, first by the Gendarmerie Impériale, then the Gendarmerie Royale de Paris.

In 1830, the Garde Municipale was created and subsequently disbanded in 1848. The Garde Civique, which was formed at this time, was not to last long either, as the Garde Républicaine was founded in June. It was comprised of an infantry regiment and a cavalry regiment. The first president of the French Republic, Louis Napoleon Bonaparte, made the Garde a permanent part of the Gendarmerie in 1849.

Changes in its name and organizational structure have never called into question its essential role. During the Second Empire regime, it was known as the Garde de Paris. On September 4 1870, the National Defense cabinet would once more give it the name Garde Républicaine, which it still bears today.

During the First World War a third of its forces were sent to the front to fight as part of the army. 222 Gardes would fall in the line of duty. In 1926, the Garde's flag and standard would receive the Croix de Chevalier of the Legion of Honour from President Doumergue.

During the Occupation, many members of the Garde fought in the Resistance as part of the "Saint-Jacques" network led by Colonel Vérines, who was shot in 1943 in Cologne. After the Liberation, the Garde was named the Garde Républicaine de Paris. It fought in the war in Indochina, and was awarded the Military Cross. The inscription "Indochina 1945-1954" was added to the Garde's emblems.

In 1978, the Garde was reorganized and its missions redefined. The infantry regiment was split into two regiments that would each receive separate missions. On November 11 1979, President Valéry Giscard d'Estaing presented flags to both infantry regiments, thus officializing this reform.

Today the Garde Républicaine's purpose is to assure the security and honor of the institutions and highest state authorities of the French Republic. It may also, at the discretion of the Minister of Defense, be called upon to help maintain order in Paris. It receives special missions which require specific means, such as mounted surveillance of the forests or motorcycle escorts for national or international sporting events. It participates in the public relations operations for the Gendarmerie with the help of its special formations.

The Garde Républicaine is an elite corps which is closely linked to the life of the nation, and adds to the glory of grand occasions which mark the history of France. A repository for the great traditions of the prestigious French Army corps which have succeeded one another over the centuries, the Garde Républicaine carries on this august heritage. Its great veneration and respect for tradition and its originality, as expressed in the specificity of its missions, make the Garde the quintessential instrument for furthering the aims of the highest institutions of the French Republic.

The Cavalry Band on Bastille Day

As the cavalry band musicians parade down the Champs-Elysées they execute an escort trot. In the foreground is the drummer, the only band member who leads his horse with foot-reins. The biggest drum is a bass B flat and the smallest a treble E flat; they are attached to a cradle-like metal armature with a ring that fits into the pommel of the saddle.

Racing

The enthusiasm elicited by horse racing goes back to the dawn of time. As soon as humans had mastered riding and harnessing techniques, their natural penchant for competition spurred them to pit their horses against one another. Accounts have come down to us of races held for the first Olympic games in ancient Greece in 776 BC. But it was during the Roman Empire that equestrian competitions reached their apogee. The hippodromes had a track that was 775 yards long, with a hairpin turn at each end. Teams of four horses called quadriga would compete, coming within a hairsbreadth of one another as they careened dangerously around the curves.

Passions became so enflamed among the thousands of spectators gathered together on the stadium tiers that sometimes riots would break out. In the time of the Byzantine Empire, one race actually turned into a civil war, with several thousand dying in the turmoil. As a result, the Emperor Justinian had to take such drastic measures that the games eventually became obsolete.

Other races were held but they were only organized occasionally and had no fixed rules. The English were the first to develop and codify rules for horse racing, which became customary during the 18th century. A key date for racing is the inauguration of the Jockey Club in 1750. The aim of this parent organization was to coordinate all the races that were held in Great Britain. In France, after episodes such as Prince d'Haricourt's challenge to Monsieur de Marsan in 1664 on the Saint-Germain plains, racing would develop rapidly with the founding of the Société d'Encouragement in 1833. A French Jockey Club was founded in 1835. The first official races were held at the Champs de Mars and at Chantilly. Longchamp was not opened until 1857, and at the time all races were run at a gallop. In order to encourage obstacle racing, the Society of Steeple-Chases of France was created in 1864. After many bitter administrative disputes, the Société d'Encouragement for improving French half-bred horses codified trotting racing. At the time the most important equestrian trials were all held on French soil.

Weighing-in at Saint-Cloud

During the 19th century, just as today, at certain equestrian events the spectacle in the stands is every bit as riveting as on the racetrack itself. Spectators rival one another in elegance, while horses and jockeys arduously vie with one another to defend the colors of their owners.

Harness Racing

The first harness or trotting races took place in France in the early 19th century. Horses harnessed to light sulkies competed on the Western and Northern beaches of France. It took considerable insistence on the part of enthusiasts for trotting racing competitions to be officially recognized by the administrations concerned, such as the Haras Nationaux and the Ministry of Agriculture.

Trotting races are usually ridden harnessed, but there are also monté races, i.e. races ridden under saddle, especially in France. As opposed to the United States where most horses are Pacers, in France race horses are predominately Trotters. They are specially trained to extend their trot as far as possible without breaking into a canter. A horse that breaks into a canter in a race is penalized. There are always many competitors. The distances covered vary from between 2515 to 2843 yards. Most competitions are held in wintertime. The most fervent aficionados of this sport meet at the Vincennes racetrack where the famous Prix International d'Amerique closes the season. Having won all the most important races, sometimes several years in a row, certain French Trotters like Une de Mai, Idéal du Gazeau, and Ourasi are already certain to go down in the annals of history. Watching the horses pulling their sulkies at break-neck speed and moving with perfectly streamlined, almost mechanical ease, their mouths foaming, is truly exhilarating. It is no wonder there are so many ardent admirers and supporters of these sporting events.

Although the pari-mutuel betting system and the lure of winning have now become inextricably tied to racing, it must be remembered that its initial purpose still remains the improvement of horse breeds. Holding these meets gives employment to thousands of people. Many more people attend and encourage horse racing out of love for the sport rather than in hopes of winning money.

There are a number of equestrian statues which pay homage to great champions, such as the famous sculpture *Gladiateur* at the gates of Longchamp - one more proof that races have not lost their reason for being: it is a glorification and veneration of the horse through its power and speed.

A Trotter training

The main goal in the training of a Trotter is to develop his musculature, his breathing and to lengthen his stride. The areas covered are progressively extended and marked periodically with speed marks called "bout-vite".

Obstacle Racing

Obstacle races are always very spectacular. The horses and jockeys must not only master great speed but also great skill in jumping. There are distinctions to be made among hurdle racing, steeplechase, and cross-country steeplechase.

In hurdle racing, the obstacles, or fences, are 41 inches high and 39 inches wide and made of simple branches. There are seven fences placed at periodic intervals over the course of the 2734 - 3281 yard track. Steeplechase gets its name from races once held in villages in which horsemen had to ride as fast as possible from one village's church tower to another, galloping through the fields and jumping over any obstacles in their paths. Today this trial covers 3281 yards, with at least eight fences, four of which must be of different shapes, placed at periodic intervals. These races are essentially held at racetracks. There are, however, still cross-country steeplechase races held in the countryside on marked trails.

Because of the tremendously arduous exertion required of horses for hurdle racing, they only begin their careers at the age of three. Steeplechase fences are often intimidatingly high and can be widely different in appearance and make-up, e.g. brick or stone walls, rivers, fences, ditches or hurdles. This is a risky enterprise for both horse and jockey, and falls are common.

The Auteuil racetrack, on the outskirts of the Bois de Boulogne in Paris, is the French Mecca for this type of racing. The fences are particularly high and separated by long straight-aways. In contrast, the fences at the Enghien racetrack are lower but more numerous and require more technique; in the end they are more difficult for both the jockey and his mount.

In France the most important obstacle racing events are: the Grand course de Haies, the Prix du Président de la République, the Grand Steeple, the Prix Murat, the Haye-Jousselin and the Prix des Drags, which is traditionally enlivened by a magnificent parade of horse-drawn carriages with the drivers and passengers all dressed in grand style.

Flatracing

Flatracing horses begin their careers at two years of age, at which time they are not allowed to enter too many races to avoid wear and tear on their still-developing bodies. The flatrace horse is at the height of his career at the age of three. Generally horses of the same sex and age compete against one another. There are certain trials however that enable flatracing horses of different ages to compete. Distances covered vary from about 1,300 yards to 5,250 yards for the famous Prix de Gladiateur. The distance of the average race, however, is between 2,300 and 2,740 yards.

In France, flatracing competition are held from May to October every year. The most prestigious trials are held at the Maisons-Laffitte, Longchamp, Deauville, Saint-Cloud and Chantilly racetracks. There are also less important meets that take place at smaller racetracks in the provinces. Among the most famous flatracing races are the Prix du Jockey-Club, the Grand Prix de Paris, and of course the Prix de l'Arc de Triomphe, held in October at Longchamp.

While the majority of flatraces are reserved for Thoroughbreds, there are also some races held for half-bred horses as well. The highly reputed Anglo-Arab races are held every year at the racetrack of the Pompadour studfarm.

Each racetrack has its unique characteristics which have an influence on the outcome of the race. For example, Longchamp has a very long slope which often comes as a surprise to horses approaching it for the first time. The two kilometer strightaway at Maisons-Laffitte is clearly to the advantage of long-distance and endurance horses. The state of the course is also a determining factor: some horses perform better than others on sodden or heavy ground, while others reach their maximum capacity on dry or light ground.

A timeless ceremony

From the weighing-in of the jockeys to the presentation of the horses, the preparation for a race follows an immutable ritual well-known to racegoers. The only people allowed in the presentation circle with the horses are their owners, who are instantly recognizable by their light colored suits and top hats.

The jockeys, who receive their last coaching before the race, proudly sport the colors of their racing stables on their blouses. The racegoers thoroughly scrutinize the horses' behavior before the race to help them make last minute betting decisions. They take into consideration the horses' past history, their performance during the last race, but also the renown of the trainers and jockeys.

The physical condition of the horse and the skill of the jockey play a vital role in the outcome of the race. The sight of the lead horses galloping wildly,

vying with one another to get on the inside, and the extraordinary effort and speed involved arouses unbridled enthusiasm among the crowd. The suspense remains undiminished until the last few yards before the finishing post. All the owners, spectators, and racegoers, whether on the grass or in the stands, are excited by the stakes and scream to encourage their favorite horse. Often at the end of the race they burst into shouts of joy or disappointment. But it is all quickly forgotten as they get ready to place new bets and hurry to exchange predictions on the next race.

The Prix de Diane

The Grand Prix de Diane, organized by the company Hermès and traditionally held the second Sunday of June at Chantilly, is exclusively reserved for three year old fillies. This flatrace covers a distance of 2296 yards.

Show-jumping

The equestrian discipline known as show-jumping was not officially recognized until the second half of the 18th century. Horses used to be taught to jump for the Hunt, clearing hedges, fences or tree trunks which were obstacles in their paths.

It is certainly in Ireland, home of the steeplechase, that show-jumping had its beginnings. At the time, jumping competitions were either for height or length. Disciples of the Hunt who wanted to acquire a horse were thus able to judge its ability and style. Progressively these competitions became a sport in their own right. In 1875, the Ecole de Cavalerie de Saumur added some jumping to its public performances of the Haute Ecole. The first international show-jumping competition was held in 1907 at the Olympia stadium in London.

At the behest of a Swede by the name of Count Von Rosen, this equestrian discipline became part of the Olympic Games in Stockholm in 1912, as did dressage and combined training competitions. Although the basis for the F.E.I. (International Equestrian Federation) was established in 1912, it was not until after World War II that show-jumping competitions, or Concours Hippiques as they are also known, developed significantly.

Today show-jumping is by far the most popular equestrian sport after horseracing, in terms of both spectators and participants. The advantages of this sport are that it is easily understood by the uninitiated spectator and that it is full of suspense until the very last minute. Here more than ever, horse and rider must meld into one to be able avoid pitfalls and jump over any manner of obstacles in one bound. The skill, mastery, and concentration of the rider, and the obedience, suppleness, and power of the jumping horse are tested to their utmost.

A show-jumping competition is by tradition always held in full dress. Fair play is the rule of the day. Contestants rarely challenge the verdict of the judges on a bar that has been knocked over or how much time has elapsed. The regulation clothing for riders is strict: dark or scarlet blazers, light riding jodhpurs and the obligatory dark or black riding hat. There are several judges on the course for each competition. The fences are colorful and often decorated in a lively, original way. Most fences are made of horizontal wooden bars resting on supports at each end. The height of the fences varies depending on the level of the competition.

There are several types of fences that can be put into two different categories: high or upright fences, made of bars or stockade fencing all placed on the same plane at variable heights. Walls can also be included in this category: i.e. obstacles built up of wooden blocks that a horse can easily knock over. A spread, as its name suggests, is a fence that spreads outward horizontally over several parallel planes. The most common fences are known as oxers, which are made of two high fences with a short interval between them that the horse must jump over in a single bound. A progressive or ramped oxer is an oxer in which the front bar is lower than the rear bar, whereas a straight oxer's front and rear bars are at the same level. Lastly, a triple bar is a fence with a succession of three sets of bars which become progressively higher.

All these fences are purposely built to fall apart easily. The horse can knock them over without risk of injury. Obstacles may be isolated or placed close to one another in groups of two or three; these are called double or triple. Most of the time they should be jumped in a set order. There are, however, some free choice competitions in which the rider can choose the order him or herself.

When there is a jumpoff, the horses and riders who have obtained a clear round once again find themselves on the same course. Certain fences may be taken away or made higher. The criteria used to decide the outcome are the fastest time and fewest penalties incurred. During a *puissance* competition, the riders must jump over several fences and a wall whose height is raised by several inches after each clear round. Just as in pole vault jumping, in this discipline records are beaten on a regular basis.

**Eric Navet
on Quito de Baussy**

Eric Navet, winner of the world show-jumping championship in August 1990 in Stockholm, is a breeder as well as a horseman. His major asset is the horse Quito de Baussy, bred by Navet himself, who is a descendant of a great line of Selle Français and the sire for the family stud farm.

Dressage Competition

Orchestrated like a ballet, the dressage competition is certainly the most esthetic and harmonious of equestrian disciplines. Dressage figures are evocative of dance, figure skating and gymnastics. Introduced only in the 20th century, dressage spread outside of the small circle of Haute Ecole horsemen and initiates to reach a wider audience. The main objective of dressage is absolute harmony between the rider and his or her mount. The day of the competition, no effort is spared in grooming the horse's coat till it gleams, and plaiting his mane perfectly, so he looks his best. Horsemen and women take great care in their dress as well, and wear a top hat, dark jacket, white riding jodhpurs and impeccably shined riding boots.

The ceremony begins with a moment of utter silence and reverence. After a period of warming up and loosening up in the paddock, the first contestant makes a grand entrance into the ring, which is either sand or grass; it is always perfectly flat and delineated by low painted wooden rails. Letters painted on the small side panels act as landmarks for the figures to be executed. The exercises are done in order of increasing difficulty, in accordance with the level of the competition.

Voltes, half-voltes, serpentines, circles and diagonals follow one after another in graceful, lofty transitions from trot, collected canter, passage to piaffe. Jury members are seated in different locations around the ring and evaluate the elegance of the horse and rider as one entity: their ease, the impulsion of the mount, the precision of the paces, the seat and balance of the rider as well as the judicious, delicate use of aids (the movements of the calves and hands used to lead the horse and regulate his speed). The horse must appear entirely submissive, but in no way constrained, and should never strain against the reins. He should face forward when moving straight ahead, and when riding a turn should make a length bend in the direction of that circle. His gaits must be thoroughly regular and his movements poised and smooth. This accomplishment requires rigorous training, enormous sensitivity and knowledge of animal psychology as well as being able to move with great finesse and grace.

As opposed to flatracing, whose rules are easy for any spectator to understand, dressage competitions usually attract an audience of aficionados that is necessarily more limited. It is indeed quite difficult for a newcomer to the discipline to judge and fully appreciate the difficulty, delicacy, and purity of these performances. All the same, the beauty of the horses and riders moving with such harmony is obvious to every viewer. Certain horses, like the Andalusian and Lipizzaner, have a naturally elevated gait and are perfectly suited for this sort of trial. But in the hands of an excellent dressage rider, any horse with good conformation can hope to attain the highest heights of the discipline.

The achievements of two famous horsewomen, Dominique d'Esmée and Margit Otto-Crépin have proved this point beautifully. The qualifications of the horse are very important, but those of the trainer and horseman or woman are primordial. According to their results and their performance in competition, dressage riders are classified into several categories. There are seven reprises, or successions of increasingly difficult figures and exercises, adapted to each level. Some are reserved for local competitions, others for regional or national competitions. Only the best horsemen and women participate in international competitions, such as the Prix Saint-Georges, the F.E.I. Intermédiaire 1 and 2, and the Grand Prix Spécial, a reprise that lasts 7 minutes 30 seconds and is the most advanced and difficult of all.

A *kür* competition allows for much greater freedom of execution and creativity; it is a choreographed riding performance given to the accompaniment of music chosen by the horseman or woman. This marvelous ballet gives the illusion of perfect accord between the rider, the horse and the music. The figures are entirely free and in harmony with the score. The horseman or woman is thus able to express his or her sensibility.

The judges take into consideration the performance from a technical standpoint as well as the overall impression.

Margit Otto-Crépin

The natural elegance and mastery of Margit Otto-Crépin are in perfect harmony with the dressage discipline at which she excels. She was European Dressage Champion in 1987 and won the silver medal at the Olympics in Seoul on the Holsteiner Corlandus, son of a Selle Français.

Eventing

Eventing is the competition which brings together the greatest number of equestrian disciplines. It has various phases, including trials for dressage, consistency, steeplechase, cross-country and show-jumping. At one time these tests were used for selecting horses for the cavalry. This is why eventing used to be called "the Military". Today it is open to all horsemen or women who have a competition permit. As the horses undergo these very strenuous trials, they must demonstrate their manageability, the harmony and elegance of their turnout overall, as well as their endurance and jumping ability. The trials take place over a three day period; officially called a "Three Day Event", they have come to be known simply as "eventing". As some of the trials require water, competitions generally take place in open countryside near large expanses of water and wooded areas.

The first day

The first day is devoted to the dressage phase. This discipline requires that the contestants execute, in a standard ring, a succession of set figures at a walk, trot and canter. The judges give points for purity of style, precision, the harmony of horse and rider, and the way they move and execute the figures, as well as the horse's impulsion, skill and rhythm.

The second day

The second day is the most trying. It is ridden in wide open fields and offers the spectators the chance to spend the whole day in contact with nature. The endurance, tenacity, and mastery of the competitors are put to the test. This phase begins with a long-distance trial in which the horse and rider must cover a distance of about two and a half to three miles, riding along paths and trails full of bumps and hollows. Usually these trials are done at a trot, whose average speed should be approximately 10 mph. It is a test of consistency, not a race. The horseman or woman does not try to be the fastest but to keep as close as possible to the set average, making sure to spare the horse's energy for the trials yet to come. Every second over regulation time is penalized.

A steeple-chase over a distance of some 3,400 yards follows the dressage test; horse and rider must jump over nine or ten fences like those found on a racetrack: hurdles, fences, open ditches, etc. This must be accomplished in the regulation time of 5 minutes to 5 minutes 20 seconds. Next comes a course of 3 1/2 to 4 1/4 miles which has to be covered at the same speed as the long distance trial. After each event there is a ten minute break to allow the horses to rest and recover from the intense activity, and get their strength back. A veterinarian is always on hand to make sure the horses are fit to move on to the next stage of the competition. The veterinarian's decision is final. The suspense mounts for the last trial of the day, the cross-country. Covering a distance of about 3.7 miles at around 15.4 mph, the horses and riders must jump over 22 to 30 fixed obstacles, such as walls, banks or ditches which cannot be knocked over, on extremely uneven ground. The natural materials used for constructing these obstacles gives them a rustic country look.

There are often many imposing combinations of tree-trunks, hedges and fences. The course-builder often plays with perspective to make the obstacles seem particularly intimidating. Both horses and riders take great risks and are sometimes victims of spectacular falls.

During this event, spectators most enjoy the water ditch or river obstacle, which the horse approaches with a bound and then fords, splashing water everywhere. Various obstacles can be overcome in different strategic ways. The bravest riders always take the shortest and most difficult route - successfully negotiated, it is always the fastest, and, since the time limit must be respected and all obstacles must be cleared, the most daring riders can often pick up valuable points to add to their overall score. Those who choose the less risky alternative route, will inevitably take longer. The organizers of these competitions often have a pronounced sense of theatricality, and obstacles may sometimes be in the shape of anything from a straw hut or stable stall to a picnic table.

Show-jumping Trial for the Finale

The third day

On the third day, the finale of the competition is a traditional show-jumping trial. Although they have already gone through very strenuous trials on the previous days, the horses still have to be in top shape for this event. If there are several competitors tied for first place, the third day decides among them. It proves that the horse, after having expended so much energy and physical effort, can still be in possession of all its capacities. Covering a distance of about 550 to 650 yards, the course is comprised of ten to twelve obstacles, which cannot be more than 3.9 feet high, and which must be jumped from many different directions. After this test, the performance scores for each day are added up for overall ranking. The winners are given a triumphal welcome and are now able to savor the sweet taste of victory, after their long, arduous, and painstaking training.

The Cross-country trial

In eventing the cross-country test is the most spectacular. The course is studded with many very impressive obstacles and often includes a river that must be forded.

Driving Competitions

In order to carry on the noble tradition of carriage driving, many enthusiasts participate in driving competitions.

These trials, which follow some of the same principles as eventing, consist of various tests that are held over the course of three days.

The first phase is known as presentation, and comes close to being a contest of elegance. The driver and groom are very finely dressed, the horses meticulously groomed with their coats glistening, the harness and vehicle sparkle. Most of the time the driver wears a top hat, a sharp formal suit complete with gloves and a lap apron or blanket. The slightest detail, like the cleanliness of the harness, the polish of the tack, or the harmony of the vehicle with the horses is taken into consideration. The carriages used for the presentation and dressage trials are often magnificent old two or four-wheeled coaches which have been lovingly restored. Everything gleams, from the metal wheel hoops to the lanterns, complete with their candles. The drivers are scrupulous about the perfect upkeep of their carriages and carefully restore them to be strictly authentic, even down to the choice of colors.

The horse-drawn carriages of the big stables used to be recognizable by the color of their owners' coats of arms. From a dog cart used for transporting hounds for the Hunt to magnificent tilburies and phaetons, all light carriages may compete in the presentation trial. Some modern vehicles are also used in driving competitions. As part of their overall evaluation, the judges take into consideration the safety of the equipment and the solidity of the harnesses. Several accessories, such as a knife for slicing the harness-trace in case of emergency, a halter, a swingle-tree and a spare pair of reins must be part of the equipment.

As in eventing, there is also a dressage trial. Driving competitions are in fact much like eventing, the important difference being that the horses are harnessed rather than mounted. In a ring the drivers and their teams execute a succession of set figures at a walk and a trot, making many transitions - from a

light trot, to a working trot, to an extended trot, etc. Loftiness, precision and suppleness of execution are the objectives sought after. Each contestant moves methodically from perfect circles to serpentines, to diagonals, to reining back, all in the purest style possible.

The second day of this competition is devoted to the long-distance and marathon trials. Most of the time drivers change carriages for these trials, preferring more modern, stabler vehicles with steel bodies, disk-brakes and sometimes even compressed air suspension. With a buckboard judge seated next to him, each driver covers many miles trying to stay within the time allotted and to maintain a consistent pace. It is indeed a beautiful sight to watch these

hard-working horses file by, pulling their stagecoaches and carriages from by-gone days over bumpy paths and forest trails. The marathon which follows the long-distance test is certainly the most spectacular and therefore the most popular trial among the public.

Several obstacles are placed on the course the horses must take. The teams moving at high speed must, for example, ford rivers or streams, turn on a hillside, weave through trees and around fences. Crowded around the obstacles that are particularly hard to get around, the spectators hold their breaths, and root for the teams with warm applause. The skill of the drivers, the manageability of the horses, the suppleness and flexibility of the team as a whole are often amazingly impressive.

The competition ends on the third day with a maneuverability test. Once again taking up their shining show carriages, the drivers compete in the ring, driving around an obstacle course made up of balls balancing on pins. The objective is to clear the course as quickly as possible without knocking over any of the balls. After the trial is finished the overall rank of each contestant is established. This sport requires an enormous investment. Competitors must have two carriages, one for presentation and dressage and the other for the marathon, a beautiful harness, a team of horses and, finally, a vehicle for transporting it all. Nevertheless, the number of enthusiasts is increasing daily. Driving competitions may offer a promising future for draft horses, which are officially entitled to participate in their category.

**Presentation
of the team
of the Haras de Saintes**

Teams of three horses are unusual and difficult to handle. This is called a cross-bow team, with one tracer horse in the lead and two shaft horses behind. A tridem is a team with three horses harnessed in a line, one behind the other, and a troika has three horses harnessed side by side.

Horse-ball

**Horse-ball
demonstration at the
Horse Fair**

*The only equestrian team sport
besides polo, horse-ball in a
very physical and virile sport
which is played on a flat field
measuring at least 65.5 x 27.5
yards.*

Horse-ball takes its inspiration from a sport known as pato lorrain, as well as from rugby and basketball. It is a relatively new equestrian sport which was created in 1976 in the South-west of France during a riding club event. Six horsemen, two who act as replacements, are pitted against one another, in an attempt to capture a ball with six leather handles that make it easier to catch and to pass. Each team's objective is to score as many goals as possible at the other team's expense. The goals are somewhat like basketball hoops, except that the baskets are a yard in diameter and placed at a height of 10 feet. There are two ten minute breaks, with a half-time pause for the teams to change sides: horse-ball action is very fast. Players on the same team must pass the ball three times before scoring a goal. No rider may keep the ball for more than 30 seconds. Players continually try to surprise and fool the opposing players by coming to abrupt stops, speeding up suddenly, pulling away in a violent burst of speed, and changing directions sharply.

The ideal mount for this sport is rather small, because players often have to bend down to pick up the ball from the ground. This small horse must also have a fiery, spirited temperament but still be easy to handle. Camargues, Spanish and Arabian horses are favorites for horse-ball. They are trained very methodically, in much the same way as American Quarter Horses or Camargues who are to be used for rounding up cattle. It often happens that in the heat of the action

the horseman drops the reins. It is most interesting to watch how thoroughly the horse becomes involved in the game, and is even able to anticipate offense and defense action.

The rules for horse-ball were rather unclear in the early days but have now become codified to minimize brutal or dangerous behavior that might harm the horses or the riders. This sometimes rather tough contact sport requires horses and horsemen to wear protective gear: helmets with chinstraps, padded shirts for the players, and rubber athletic supporters for the horses. Players are not allowed to touch one another or hold each other back by their uniforms. They may not block the other players' path on purpose either. The umpire, also on horseback, calls a penalty by blowing a whistle, at which point a free penalty shot is granted to the opposing team. Return to play works as it does in rugby. The player who arrives first has priority to pick up the ball. When two players are fighting over the ball, the umpire separates them and orders a throw-in. Horse-ball is now played by many people and, even in France, it has become very popular. Every year there is a French championship and games are held in different categories with the best teams competing. More and more horse-ball seems to be played as an interlude to fill in the gaps between other equestrian competitions, and its popularity is spreading in other countries such as Belgium, Germany and Wales.

Hunter Trials

Hunter trials are very popular in the United States and are gaining in popularity in France as well. Competitions include three trials for judging style and turnout. The first points are awarded for overall presentation. Great importance is placed on the appearance of the horse as well as that of the rider.

This is why horsemen and women whose turnout is particularly refined are given many bonus points. Traditional competition clothing is considered too conservative and not original enough. The horse is groomed until his coat gleams, his harness is polished to a shine, his tail is beautifully braided and his mane is plaited. Some contestants go so far as to match the color of their saddle with the horse's coat. The slightest detail is taken into account and has an impact on the judges.

The judges then evaluate the horse and rider on flat ground. The poise of the horse as he moves, his willingness and concentration are taken into consideration, as are the rider's seat, balance, bearing and the adjustment of the reins. During this demonstration, horse and rider must give the impression of being one. The contestant's heels should be low, with his or her legs in a natural position. The rider's weight should be evenly distributed, the body remaining motionless so as not to shift the center of gravity. The hands should be a certain distance apart just in front of the saddle, with the fingers and arms all correctly positioned. The horse should seem completely calm and submissive and should not strain at his reins, although he must have enough impulsion to propel him well forward. The action of his gaits must seem smooth, effortless and extended, with sufficiently high strides.

It is not a succession of dressage figures, but nonetheless all the basic principles of equitation must be scrupulously respected in order to obtain a certain harmony, as well as the optimum efficiency in the use of natural aids: e.g. the seat, calves, reins, and the weight of the body.

The last trial is a small obstacle course. The obstacles are never very high, usually about the same height as natural obstacles one would encounter in a forest. Before entering the obstacle course, the rider canters around the ring in a circle.

Once in the ring, the rider must maintain his or her horse at the same gait without breaking the rhythm or cadence. The horse must seem light and supple and jump over all the obstacles, gathering just the right momentum. The trajectory of the jump should form a perfect half circle. Touching down should be graceful and orderly. The rider's position and movements are also very important; he or she should lean neither too far forward nor too far backward. Hunter trials adhere strictly to basic equestrian techniques.

French Championship at Fontainebleau

Hunter trials were originally inspired by the equitation once practiced by English Lords for the Hunt. The aim is not jumping over high or difficult obstacles, but jumping with the best style possible. Above is the elegant Marie Courrèges jumping in a hunter trial.

Polo

Polo is a sport all about motion and finesse which emphasizes the natural abilities and beauty of the horse in action. Rapidity, coordination and sportsmanship are the principle characteristics of this equestrian game, which is one of the oldest in the world.

The origins of polo date back to ancient times. The first written accounts of polo date back to the time of Darius I, king of the Persians, 522-486 BC. Thanks to conquests and trade the sport spread throughout Asia, especially in China, Japan and India. English colonizers in India for the tea trade discovered a polo-like game known as kangjai. The people of Manipur near the Burmese border would meet on the village square to play kangjai, riding small indigenous ponies and using mallets and a ball. It was a violent, often brutal game with few rules. But then, as today, the purpose of the game was to propel the ball between the opposing team's goalposts. Faithful to their ancestral traditions, even today the peoples of the Manipur region still meet every year to hold kangjai games. According to some experts, the name polo comes from the *pulu*, a Tibetan plant whose root was used for making the balls.

The game was appropriated and transformed by the English colonial aristocracy and British army officers stationed in India. The Silchar Polo Club was the first polo club, and was founded in 1859. Any behavior or attitude that might cause harm to the opposing team was forbidden, guidelines for hitting the ball were established, and the first official rules were set down in 1875. Ten years later the sport made its way to Europe during a demonstration by British cavalry officers home from the colonies.

Polo is played on flat, grassy turf, measuring 300 by 160 yards. Paddock polo, however, can be played on a much smaller field, for example in an indoor ring. The goalposts are placed at a height of 3.2 yards and at a distance of 8.2 yards from each other at both extremities of the field. They are designed to fall down when hit hard. The ball is made of poplar wood or plastic, measures 3 1/2 inches in diameter and weighs no more than 4 3/4 oz. The mallet is 4 feet 2 inches long with a bamboo handle and a cigar-shaped head. Polo is a very physical, risky game, and both horseman and rider must wear protective equipment. Teams are made up of four players each; the first two play offence. The center forward player is the key player on the team and is often the team captain or the best player; he coordinates the plays. Only one horsemen plays backfield and guards the goal. There are two umpires, one on horseback who keeps pace with the action closely, and another who judges from the sidelines. Two officials are in charge of checking on the goals scored, one stationed behind each of the goals. A player may not block the path of an opposing player. Depending upon the level of the match, the game has six to eight periods, known as "chukkers", which last seven minutes each. As almost the entire time the ball is in play the horses are galloping, they are forced to expend so much energy that players change horses at each break. This means that every team member has to have four horses.

Polo was introduced into the United States by James Gordon Bennett, who was owner of the famous New York Herald newspaper. After a visit to Great Britain, he put together his own team. From 1886 on, the English and Americans played against one another for the famous Westchester Cup. Today the very wealthy town of Palm Beach is a polo mecca where the best international teams meet and play one another.

Since the time that Tom Preston introduced polo into Argentina, it has become enormously popular there. The fact that Argentina boasts many local horse breeders and that there are the pampas which stretch out as far as the eye can see, make it the perfect country for polo. There are more than 5,000 polo players and 200 polo clubs in Argentina. It is therefore not surprising that since 1933 Argentinian players are the best in the world. The largest international polo meet, the Open de Palermo, is held every year in Buenos Aires.

Polo has been played in France since 1890 in Paris at the Bois de Boulogne on the Bagatelle grounds. The suspense-filled national matches are still held there to this day, during the last weekend in August. Deauville also hosts the famous and much sought-after Coupe d'Or. Charles, Prince of Wales, is one of the personalities who can often be spotted there; he is an ardent polo enthusiast and plays on the Diables Bleus team himself. All the French teams play under the aegis of the Union des Polos de France, including the six international-level teams.

Just as in horse-ball, Polo ponies should be small in size, but extraordinarily energetic. The horses most often used are of Argentinian origin, which came out of cross-breeding between Thoroughbreds and indigenous breeds long ago. The polo match is the ultimate test of a horse's stamina, balance, and speed.

This cross-breeding produced horses which have great endurance and speed, and a playful yet competitive spirit. Often the horses participate very actively in the game, and do not only follow but also anticipate the action of the game.

Captured in the pampas where they are raised in semi-liberty, two-year-old polo ponies are handed over to *domadores* who break them in quickly and somewhat brutally. From then on, their training is specifically geared toward polo by *petisseros*, who take them through a strenuous workout and teach them to turn and change direction quickly.

The *petissero* is to polo what the stable-boy is to racing: a horseman who takes care of, grooms , exercises and loosens up the horse before handing him over to the player. It takes about four full years for a polo pony to be perfectly trained. Some of these horses are sold for astronomical prices at auctions.

A very ancient and little known sport

During polo matches the horses are particularly vulnerable to getting hit by the mallets. This is why they wear leg protectors. Any attitude or maneuver which might be dangerous for the other horses or players is strictly forbidden and incurs penalties.

Trick riding

Unlike their German and American counterparts, very few French riders practice trick riding. This is rather a pity, because trick riding is a marvelous discipline which harmoniously sets off the grace of both horse and rider.

Trick riding originally comes out of gymnastic exercises practiced in cavalry schools to make soldiers and officers more flexible. The Cossacks, a famous horse-riding people, also used to do exercises on horseback while galloping, in order to trick their adversaries and dodge projectiles as they were charging. These warrior exercises are part of what is known as *djighite* or Cossack trick riding. The Greeks and Romans also used to give performances in which riders would do acrobatics on the back of a horse or bull. There are some frescoes, notably in Crete, which bear witness to these events.

Today trick riding is closer to gymnastics. In addition to the impressive physical performance of the rider, beauty and perfection in the movements and precision in the transitions are the sought-after objectives. This equestrian discipline is very popular among children and teenagers, and it is an excellent way for them to overcome their fear of the horse as they concentrate on the various figures to be performed. Often before they do the exercises on an actual horse, they practice first on a pommel horse. Next they learn how to stand on the horse's croup and to do various jumps and figures.

Several types of trick riding

There are several types of trick riding. There is academic trick riding for competition, in which the horse or a stand-in pony is turned on the lunge in a circle at a gallop. A two-handled surcingle girth is placed on the horse's back for the riders to hold on to. A good trick riding horse must be very calm and patient under all circumstances. It is extremely important that he be able to gallop with a perfectly consistent gait and be very comfortable. Finally, he must be strong and robust enough to bear the weight of three trickriders, and spirited enough to always keep up the same rhythm. In circus trick riding the horse is let loose on a circular track so several other horses can follow him. Trick riders or circus riders will do a series of thrilling, daredevil feats before the clamoring crowd. Just as in figure skating, there are two types of trick riding trials: one of required figures and the other free figures. Teenagers less than eighteen participate in competitions in teams of three, and adults individually.

Six official figures

There are six required figures. The jury judges the quality and harmony of execution. To do a *figure à cheval*, the rider takes a running jump onto the horse in motion, and ends up sitting on the horse's back. He or she then lets go of the girth handles, stretches his or her arms out horizontally and jumps to dismount. In the *étendard position*, the trickrider kneels down on the horse's back stretching the left arm out in front and the right leg behind, then dismounts just as above.

For the *moulin*, the seated rider does a complete turn, swinging both legs, one at a time, first over the horse's neck and then over his croup. The rider comes back to his or her original position in four moves. *Amazone* and *ciseaux* are the same sort of required figures.

The most spectacular and dangerous figure by far is *standing*. The rider first kneels on the horse's back then slowly stands up using his or her outstretched arms for balance.

Free figures

Points are awarded for the free figure trial based to a large extent on the esthetic quality of the figures and transitions. It is like a ballet which is often quite original and requires a real artistic sensibility and perfect synchronization and coordination on the part of the rider. Like figure skating and dance, the succession of movements in trick riding is very harmonious and spectacular, especially when accompanied by music.

Trick riding in a circle

This is a free figure. In competition children under the age of eighteen compete in teams of eight. In free figure programs there can be no more than three riders on the horse's back at one time.

The Circus horse

Long after the applause dies down, children remember the marvelous circus feats and numbers they were so enchanted by. Of course, adults love to watch the exciting, colorful spectacle too. The circus originally started in the Middle Ages with tumblers or buffoons, who, like Captain Fracasse from the novel by Théophile Gautier, would give theater and acrobatics performances at fairs and marketplaces.

Experts date the origin of the circus to 1780, when Philippe Asthley, a former dragoon in the British Army, built the first circus ring on Westminster Road in London. It was soon to have competition from the Royal Circus on Blackfriars Road. As a result of Phillipe Asthley's military and equestrian past, he made the horse a central figure in the circus. There were also pantomimes and acrobatics performed on the ground, as well as many daring trick riding performances and other breathtaking equestrian demonstrations. Since that time a venerable heritage has been passed down from the many important horsemen and horsewomen whose names will go down in the annals of entertainment history. Two of these great circus dynasties, the Gruss and Knie clans, were established in France and Switzerland respectively. Their enormous tours thrilled audiences all over Europe.

It is important to remember that the circus is, above all, about the art of showmanship. The elegance of the horses, the beauty of their colorful, vividly plumed and decorated harnesses and the harmony and unusualness of their coats are therefore essential, as they help create the magical feeling of the circus. Although all breeds can be trained as circus horses, the noble, lofty bearing and elevated gait of Andalusian and Lipizzaner horses make them hands-down favorites. To create a feeling of harmony, often horses whose coats are nearly the same color are chosen to perform a number together. But of course, a circus trainer will still always select a spirited horse over a lack-luster, lackadaisical horse. Many stallions are used because they have strong personalities and often like to show off.

The choice of a mount is determined by his skills and originality rather than his bloodline. Training a circus horse is a difficult undertaking which requires an enormous amount of patience, but above all, deep knowledge of horse behavior and psychology.

There is no real school or precise method for learning this discipline. Attentive observation of a horse's natural attitudes, (e.g. rearing, levades, and lying down) and his own particular temperament make it possible to develop specific training perfectly adapted to each horse.

Gradually these exercises become increasingly sophisticated and difficult. To the great enjoyment of the audience, some horses turn into real clowns, some can gallop backwards, others can do magic tricks or take an awe-inspiring array of postures. But none of this is possible if the horses do not trust their trainers wholeheartedly. It is this trust which enables horses to overcome their fear and flight instinct. Thoroughly reassured by the presence of their trainers, circus horses manage to conquer their innate fear of heights,

of fire, and of their natural enemies. Marvelous dressage numbers have been done with lions, tigers and panthers riding on horses' backs. The horse has an excellent memory and is capable of memorizing perfectly the numbers he has been taught. A well-trained horse can repeat at will an order given with just a simple gesture or vocal intonation. Of course, these equestrian numbers are largely inspired by Haute Ecole airs, such as the *piaffer, passage, levade, croupade,* and *cabriole.* Executed simultaneously by a number of horses at a simple signal from the trainer, the effect of all these figures is indeed very spectacular. Many other figures are also practiced which run the gamut from extremely basic to the outrageously daring. The horse's training is continually improved and renewed.

The circus would not exist without these daredevil trick-riding stunts which make the audience tremble with excitement. Several riders stand on the croups of their horses and juggle a motley assortment of objects, such as pins, rings, flaming torches, knives, while others drive a galloping team of horses and execute a *Hungarian post.* They perform acrobatic acts while leading ten horses or more, form human pyramids, jump daringly from one horse to another or fly through the air turning somersaults. Some circuses use historical themes as inspiration for their shows. The famed Buffalo Bill joined Barnum and Bailey's circus near the end of his life. He staged and participated in *tableaux vivants* of bison hunting and fighting between the cavalry and the American Indians.

Unlike the Haute Ecole exercises which strive for discipline, sobriety and precision, here the main goal is to capture the marvelous spectacular aspect of each exercise. Horse and rider must both constantly bring new life to their performances.

Sometimes the oddest and most unexpected props may be used, like tables, gigantic balloons, and obstacles of every description. A passionate love of the horse is passed down from generation to generation in these great circus families. Although recently some of the great stars have passed on, young people are taking over the reins, to take their places and carry on their teachings and their memory. A bittersweet mixture of fatalism and hope, the motto of circus people will always be, "The show must go on!"

"Panem et Circenses"

The Romans demanded "bread and circuses" of Caesar, but when the horse began to be used in the circus, it was in the violent chariot races. Today circus rings are always circular, and now the role the horse plays is to entertain in a playful rather than violent way. The animals trainers present to the public are calm and often astonishing in their demonstrations of skill.

The Hunt

A sport intimately tied to the forest

The main quality of a hunting horse should be endurance, because the Hunt goes on for hours on end without the rider dismounting. The horse must also be sure-footed because the ground is often muddy and rough. The horse often has to jump over small obstacles such as tree trunks, ditches or even fences that lie across his path. Without necessarily having all the qualities required for a show-jumper, he must nonetheless be a good, solid jumper. He must also be calm at a standstill, because the rider has to wait silently for some time, listening for the hounds' barking and the sounding of the horn. In England some breeders devote themselves entirely to breeding horses for the Hunt. In France, Pure-breds which were formerly racehorses are often used, as are good Selle Français, and Anglo-Arabs, which are valued for their robustness, and even Trotters. These horses get used to the hounds very quickly and are not bothered at all by the noisy, frantic mass swarming at their hooves. It is not rare to cover a distance of more than 37 miles. Neither horse nor rider can afford to become tired out too fast. In France it is customary for hunters to let the hounds run ahead, unlike the Hunt in England in which hunters gallop as closely as possible behind them. They wait for the stag to tire itself out and for the pack of hounds to encircle him. The pace of the horsemen is fast but they almost always keep at a trot to spare their horses.

For a long time the Hunt was an exclusive privilege of the aristocracy. Kings were particularly fond of this activity which combined the pleasures of hunting with long rides through the woods. Charlemagne congratulated one of his daughters for her ardent enthusiasm for the Hunt. Already practiced in ancient times, the heyday of the Hunt was during the reign of the Bourbons.

There are more than sixty hunting teams in France, and each has its own Master of the Hounds, a calling that is often handed down from father to son. Each team can be distinguished by its costume, usually inspired by a coat of arms. The Master of the Hounds leads the hunt and gives orders to the whippers-in, who control the hounds.

The Hunt always adheres to the same strict ceremony. The day before the Hunt is to take place, one or more hunt servants search the forest to locate the trail of a deer or wild boar. Before the Hunt begins, they report back to the Master of the hounds, who then decides which direction to go in.

Once the hunt servants are all assembled, the hounds and riders all come together at the meet, the place fixed upon the day before by the Huntsman. The first whipper-in stays at the front of the pack of hounds while another follows behind to make sure the dogs stay together. If the scent is fresh enough, the Hunt begins, and the hounds whose job it is to locate the prey are let loose. Once they are on the deer's track the rest of the pack is released. Often the deer tries to shake off his assailants by backtracking or running along other deer trails so they will lose his scent.

The horse is used as a simple method of locomotion for following the hounds, which chase after the large game animal in a pack. In France, among the six dog breeds used for the Hunt are the Grand Bleu de Gascogne, the Billy, and the Levesque.

The huntsmen are often very experienced and are able to determine the animal's age just by his tracks or his droppings. Cervidae, or animals in the deer family, lose their antlers every spring. The antlers always grow back larger than the year before and in a particular shape. The antlers also help determine the deer's age. The young deer is called a fawn, then at two

a young stag, or brocket. If the deer survives the Hunt it will become what is called a ten-point stag. The deer is the most regal inhabitant of the forest, and is rightly considered to be a noble animal. Its imposing stature and courage often arouse our admiration.

Certain old dogs accompany the pack as leaders. They have learned from experience to always follow the same scent trail. The deer leaves a very strong odor behind him, which in the Hunt is known as "the sentiment". When they have found the scent trail, the hounds all begin to bark, and the huntsmen and followers know which way to ride and join in the chase.

One of the unforgettable elements of the Hunt is no doubt the magnificent sound of the hunting horn ringing out, which, from the attack to the kill, informs the horsemen about the Hunt and its evolution. Every melody has its own specific meaning. The first huntsman who spots the deer blows his horn, and if he is able to see the antlers, intones how old it is. Another melody indicates that the hounds are on the right track. It sometimes happens that the pack hesitates and the younger dogs take off along the wrong trail. The whippers-in ride past them and round them up once again to lead them back to the point where they went astray. Once more on the right track, the horn is blown again. When the deer becomes completely exhausted it often finally just lies down or lets the hounds surround it. At this point the whippers-in hurry to the spot and sound the kill. One of the huntsmen or the whippers-in then gives the coup de grace with a dagger. The stag's entrails are then flung to the dogs as a reward and the horn is blown once more.

The Hunt may seem cruel to some, but it is important to realize that when an area is overpopulated with deer, they wreak havoc on surrounding farmlands. Some people prefer the Hunt as it is practiced in Germany: The hounds and horses follow a horseman dragging a cow stomach behind him. He acts like a real game animal, and takes malicious pleasure in backtracking, crossing streams and the like in order to confound the pack and the followers. There are no animals killed at the end of the day.

HORSES AND ART

Famous Horses

The Lady and the Unicorn

The unicorn is a mythical animal depicted in the Middle Ages with the body of a gelded horse, cloven hooves, and one long twisted horn coming out of its forehead. This ferocious beast could not be approached or dominated except by a young maiden. The unicorn had a beautiful ivory horn that was highly sought after for the magical and medicinal properties attributed to it and for its rarity. In reality the unicorn's horn was none other than the solitary canine tooth of a sea mammal known as the narwal. The seamen who knew the true origin of the unicorn kept it a well-guarded secret, preferring to let people believe it really existed, as no-one had ever seen one except Marco Polo, who left behind a fantastical description. The mystery surrounding this beautiful animal helped keep the price of the horn extremely high. Collectors of the time agreed to pay phenomenal sums for their Curiosity Cabinets- and they still do today. Another tapestry, just as famous as the Lady and the Unicorn, is the Bayeux Tapestry of Queen Mathilde which depicts scores of horses. Like an ancient cartoon, it tells the history of the conquest of England by William the Conqueror. One of the last scenes of this masterpiece shows the end of the battle of Hastings where the harnesses of the Norman knights' horses are so faithfully rendered.

.According to Greek mythology, the first horse was the famous Pegasus, who was engendered by Poseidon, and born out of the Medusa's chopped-off head. Riding this superb winged horse, Bellerophon wanted to fly to Olympia, the dwelling-place of the Gods. To punish his presumptuousness, Zeus sent a horsefly down to sting Pegasus' croup in mid-flight, causing him to catapult his rider into the void.

Phaeton, son of Helios, died in almost the same way after being struck by lightning because he had spirited away the chariot of the sun, which was drawn by celestial steeds whom Zeus used to chase away the clouds and provoke storms.

The fruit of the imagination of foot soldiers who were confronted for the first time with warriors on horseback, Centaurs were half-man and half-horse, and were described in mythology as creatures whose behavior was particularly bestial. Only the Centaur Chiron, Achilles' tutor, was wise and knowledgeable. The Centaurs lived in Thessaly and were massacred by Hercules, Nestor and Theseus after a banquet given by the King of Lapithes. After having tried to steal away the wife of Hercules, the famous Centaur Nessus, mortally wounded and suffering terribly, told her to take his skin, make a tunic out of it and to give it to her husband to make him more faithful. Hercules put it on and died a horrible agonizing death from poisoning.

The Amazons, the mythical tribe of women warriors and conquerors, were credited with founding the cities of Smyrna and Ephesus, among others. They supposedly burned their daughters' right breasts so they would be better at archery and are credited with inventing riding side-saddle.

The emperor Caligula, who became so demented he took himself for a god, was so enamoured of his horse that he wanted to make him a consulate. According to Roman legend, horses are born from water as they cross the tines of Neptune's trident. Neptune moved across the oceans in a chariot drawn by creatures who were half-horse half-fish. The goddess of fruitfulness, beauty and fertility, Venus also rode in a sumptuous chariot harnessed to proud white steeds who were the symbol of purity. Finally there was Athena, goddess of wisdom, the sciences and the arts, who taught humans how to ride and harness horses.

The horse is also very frequently cited in many epic stories. In The *Iliad*, Achilles had two magnificent divine horses at the siege of Troy; one named Xanthe was immortal and had the gift of speech. In order to invade the city, the Greeks pretended to give up the siege and built a gigantic wooden horse that they abandoned just outside the city, after having hidden many warriors inside its flanks. The Trojans were deceived by the subterfuge and brought the enormous wooden horse within the walls of the city, which was to be their undoing. Another mythical horse, Bucephalus, so called because he had a bull branded on his thigh, was believed to be untamable by even the greatest horseman. His master, Alexander of Macedonia, understood that his stubbornness came from the fact that he was afraid of his own shadow. He managed to make Bucephalus submit to his will by riding him facing into the sun. This notorious horse died in combat in India, and the city of Boukhephalia was named after him.

СУЗДАЛЬЦЫ

Russian Icon

These fine stylized horses are evocative of the heady times when the Christians traveled across Europe and the Middle East to take back Jerusalem. The horse was their faithful companion.

Persian Miniature

The horse was just as indispensable a companion in the opposing camp. Here, surrounding the Prophet, whose face it is forbidden to look upon, the richness of the cavalry on parade.

The Horse and Religion

The horse is a symbol of purity, especially when it has a white coat. Horses figure in many religious texts. The great Vedic tales of India make frequent references to horses.

For example, in the Rigveda, the epic story for the edification of Brahmin priests, the horses of Indra, king of the gods, master of rain and the seasons, were created from two rays of sunshine. The chariot of Surya, the sun god, is also drawn by a team of seven horses. Prince Siddhartha, who would later become the Buddha, escaped and left his home forever on the proud white steed Kanthara to meditate and preach all over India. The prophet Mohammed travelled to the heavens on El Boraq, a beautiful winged mare with the head of a woman and the body of a horse.

Closer to our culture is Saint Georges of Cappadoce, patron saint of horsemen, who freed a young virgin from the claws of a dragon. He also had a white horse with the gift of speech. There were also the four horses from the Apocalypse of Saint John: first a white horse, then a fiery red one, then a black one, and lastly a greenish-colored horse.

كه شهرنده بر كافرو ارايدى وسيد بن مغيره ديركردى
حضرتنك اولود شمسينى انك حكايتلرى كتاب اولنده

Literature

The place of the horse in literature is as important as it is in mythology and the visual arts, though quite different. If it is the horse as an animal that is most often painted, drawn and sculpted, it is the world of the horse that is generally evoked or described in literature, especially when contact between horse and horsemen took place on a daily basis. In all the writings concerning the horse, it takes part in work, travel, battle, and the favorite mode of entertainment of the upper class, the Hunt. Literature of the Middle Ages speaks of famous mounts such as Brice d'Or, who belonged to the knight Roland, and Etencedur, who belonged to the Emperor Charlemagne.

One of the most well-known was Bayard, who had magical powers and was able to bear the weight of all four sons of the Duke Aymon of Dordogne: Aalard, Renaud, Guichard and Richard. These valiant young horsemen offended Charlemagne, who pursued them as far as their castle. They were reduced to a state of poverty, gave themselves up and made amends honorably. But the Emperor took vengeance by drowning their horse in the Meuse River, with a heavy millstone tied around its neck.

Galileo had the idea of setting up a system for judging literary works in which their rhythm would be compared to horses' gaits. He believed that a good story should have a tempo close to "an Arabian horse who runs better than a hundred Friesian horses." This standard for assessing literary merit was taken up by Italo Calvino in *American Lessons*.

In the 18th century work *Natural History*, a favorite among 19th century writers, Buffon devoted one of the most famous chapters to the horse. In *La Légende des Siècles*, Victor Hugo gives the legendary prince Aymerillot de Narbonne an unforgettable pink and white horse.

Balzac's Colonel Chabert, a former Imperial cavalry officer on half-pay, is one of the most stirring portraits in *The Human Comedy*. In an altogether different vein from the *Mysteries of Paris*, Eugène Sue wrote *Arabian Godolphin, the Story of a Horse*, which told of the romantic adventures of a famous stallion, the sire of the most prestigious line of Thoroughbreds. Zola often wrote about horses in Paris; until the 20th century they had the importance cars have today but his most poignant portrayal by far is that of the horse *Bataille* who works so hard in the mines under terrible conditions.

Byron wrote the most beautiful version of the story of the legendary Polish gentleman *Mazeppa*. He had been tied naked to his Ukrainian horse by a jealous husband and managed to make his way to the Ukraine. He was to become general of the Cossacks under Peter I, who betrayed him in the end, because he wanted to become king of the Ukraine. *Mazeppa* was hanged in effigy and was forced to flee, whereupon he died a pauper in Valachy. Géricault painted several paintings about this extraordinary adventure which Victor Hugo recounted as well.

In 1815 Aragon constructed *La Semaine Sainte* around the character of Théodore Géricault, a painter who was obsessed with horses and was even one of Louis XVIII's musketeers for a time. Aragon was truly a great writer to be able to so aptly capture a world which, unlike Géricault, he had never experienced. Every horseman and woman today should read Claude Simon's *Route to Flanders*. It is a treasure trove of keen observation. Along with *Casse-Pipe* and *Le Carnet du Cuirassier Destouches*, by Céline, it is one of the best works ever written bearing testimony to the by-gone world of the mounted troops. Other lighter works stand in a category apart - there are unpretentious, humorous, and often quite touching books such as *Gaîtés de l'Escadron* by Courteline and *Souvenirs épars d'un ancien Cavalier* by Tristan Bernard.

It is perhaps not surprising that several mares in literature have such strong personalities that they are now household names, while their male counterparts often remain rather obscure. In French the name of Don Quixote's pitiful horse Rossinante has come to mean a scrawny, sickly mare with poor conformation. Another famous mare is in *Gargantua* by Rabelais. A gift of the king of Numidia to Grangousier, the father then gave the mare to his son who was sent to Paris to study. She was so enormous that the only bells Gargantua could find big enough to hang around her neck were the bells of Notre-Dame.

Toulouse-Lautrec and the world of horsemen

Even if Toulouse-Lautrec and Proust did not portray the same classes of society, they both grew up amid the same refined atmosphere in which "elegance was a duty" for horse and rider. Both Proust and Toulouse-Lautrec had occasion to admire the superb horsemen they could never be. In "Remembrance of Things Past", Proust is at a crossroads in a world where the horse is disappearing, to be replaced by the automobile. In his youth, the horse was the main mode of transportation for everyday comings and goings. The narrator describes at length an excursion in a horse-drawn carriage around the outskirts of Balbec with Madame de Villeparisis and his grandmother. The character General de Froberville was inspired by General Marquis Gaston de Gallifet, hero of one of the last great cavalry charges in history, which he led in Sedan in 1870. Prince Constantin Radziwill, one of the people the Prince de Guermantes character was based on, kept luxurious stables with equally attractive stableboys. Nadar photographed them, leaving behind an astonishing testimony to this society that disappeared forever with Marcel Proust.

The *Green Mare* is the central character in one of Marcel Aymé's novels, and *Milady* is the heroine of the novel by the same name by Paul Morand, which brings to mind the tragic destiny of her owner, Major Luc de Léal. Finally, Kessel's book *Les Cavaliers* introduced a whole new world to the West - a world that had barely changed since the time of Ghengis Khan, in which man and horse have the same fiery spirit and seem to stretch the limits of reality. Yves Courrière's book *Kessel* depicts the remarkable adventures and vicissitudes of Joseph Kessel, who made a film himself which shows the strange world of the Afghan *bouskashis*.

Sculpture

Venice: Saint Mark's Horses

This magnificent team of bronze horses probably once graced the hippodrome of Constantinople. The Crusaders brought the quadriga to Venice as part of their war booty. Unfortunately, the chariot, which is being drawn at an amble by these majestic horses, has disappeared. The work has long been attributed to Phidias. It is probably the most famous equestrian statue extant.

Since prehistoric times the horse has always been a favorite subject matter for artists. The Magdalenians of the late Paleolithic period left behind marvelous equestrian paintings and sculptures, like the whinnying horse which was discovered inside the Mas D'Azil cave, or the small polished ivory statuette found in Lourdes. There are also a number of depictions of horses carved on scrapers and other ancient bone or ivory tools. In addition to Lascaux and Niaux, there is the magnificent fresco in the Cape Blanc cave.

The Hittites and Assyrians made bas-reliefs, like that of King Assurnazirpal (883-859 BC) who is driving his chariot, drawn by three galloping horses, and hunting wild game. The Greeks also left behind many masterful bas-reliefs and sculptures depicting parades of chariots with the heroes and warriors on horseback. Two of the metopes in the Parthenon frieze represent Preparations for the Cavalcade and The Ride of the Panathenians. In 1974 in China archeologists discovered the Xian horses, an awe-inspiring life-size cavalry. They are finely sculpted, polychrome, terra-cotta portraits of the cavalrymen and their small Mongolian mounts, and are dated circa 250 BC.

To immortalize their triumphs, Roman Emperors had themselves sculpted in warlike attitudes on their horses or chariots; the bas-relief the Arch of Titus from the Roman Forum is an excellent example. The most famous triumphal monument, however, remains the Quadriga of Saint Mark in Venice. Another famous Venetian equestrian statue from the Middle

Ages is by Verrocchio. It represents the condottiere Colleone preparing for battle, his face fraught with tension, his lips tightly pursed, with a terrifying look in his eyes. Every prince in the world seems to have been immortalized on horseback: Come I de Medicis by Jean de Bologne in Florence, Charlemagne on his powerful red roan on the square of Notre Dame Cathedral, Henri IV at the Pont Neuf and Louis XIV at the Place des Victoires in Paris, Peter the Great in Saint Petersburg, to name a few. Exquisite horse-drawn carriages also often signal strategic landmarks of the great cities, such as the Brandenburg Gate in Berlin and the Arc de Triomphe du Carrousel in the Tuileries in Paris. Also in Paris, at the Place de la Concorde, there are the sumptuous horses of Marly by Coustou, the sculptor to Louis XIV and the winged horses by Coysevox, who also worked under Louis XIV.

Painting

Since the time of the Lascaux caves the horse has been a favorite subject of painters, but in the West the oldest traces of these paintings that remain are mostly from the Middle Ages. In illuminations the horse is almost always associated with war. During the Renaissance, the attitude changes and becomes much less warlike. Leonardo da Vinci drew dozens of horses in motion. Raphael in his Florentine period painted Saint George riding a "white" horse and fighting a dragon. The court portraitist Jean Clouet painted the magnificent work François I on Horseback. The Dutch animal and landscape painter Paulus Potter introduced a new note of delicacy and poetry with *The Piebald Horse*, a beautiful example of his extremely finely observed, detailed paintings. Carle Vernet stands out for his hunting and racing scenes in which the horses are particularly elegant and delicately painted. His son Horace Vernet was inspired by his travels to Algeria for his famous *Prise de Smala d'Abdel Kader*. He was one of the precursors of the 19th century romantic painters who often painted eastern horses.

Antoine Gros painted the Napoleonic conquests with great panache. Napoleon on the *Battlefield at Eylau* in the Louvre Museum is an extremely realistic depiction of the suffering of war in the cold and snow. Napoleon stands out on his mount, surrounded by his marshals. Two of Géricault's most popular paintings, also at the Louvre, are really more allegorical figures of cavalrymen in the imperial army rather than portraits. *The Officer of Mounted Chasseurs of the Guard Charging* (1812) and the *Wounded Cavalryman Leaving the Fighting* (1814) are symbolic of tragic episodes for the Empire: the first, of the onslaught of troubles after the retreat from Russia, and the second, of the French campaign and the fall of the Empire. On a completely different note, his painting of the Derby at Epsom captures the horses and jockeys in action and reinforces the notion of speed and motion through the elongation of the racers' anatomy.

Eugéne Delacroix's *Arab Fantasia* expresses the exhilaration and vitality of these proud chargers with their fiery fighting spirit. On the other hand, in Honoré Daumier's portrait of Don Quixote, the pitiful appearance of his bony Rossinante is perfect. Gustave Moreau painted at least three paintings on the theme of Diomedes' horse. One is in the Gustave Moreau Museum in Paris and another in the Museum of Rouen. Diomedes was the king of Thrace who was eaten by his own horses. He had trained them himself to attack the enemy with their teeth and fed them human flesh. Henri de Monfreid writes that this custom of keeping carnivorous horses for combat still existed among some tribes in Ethopia until the reign of the emperor Ménélik. Among modern painters, Yves Brayer in his painting *Chevaux au bord de l'Etang*, renders the Camargue region beautifully.

Pablo Picasso symbolizes apocalyptic horror through the fury of his horses in his famous painting *Guernica*. Salvador Dali and De Chirico, in their surrealist, metaphysical paintings also accord an important place to the horse. Alfred de Dreux, Edgar Degas and Raoul Dufy were specialized in painting the races and were particularly skilled at rendering the glistening colors of the jockeys' blouses, the green surroundings of the racetrack and the worldly elegance of the racegoers.

Following page
David, Napoleon Bonaparte crossing the St. Bernard Pass
On May 21, 1800, Napoleon crossed the Alps over the St. Bernard Pass, and, on June 14, fought the inconclusive battle of Marengo against the Austrians. In France, all the talk was of a dazzling victory, and this picture by David, himself a fervent "Bonapartist", is a superb piece of propaganda. The young consul joins the ranks of legendary conquerors following in the footsteps of Hannibal and Charlemagne.

ECOLE
DE
CAVALERIE.

Ch. Parrocel. In.

L. Cars Sculp.

Education d'Achilles.

Philostrates page. 289.

113

Le Pas. *Le Trot.*

Le Galop désuni du devant à droite. *Le Galop désuni du derriere à droite.*

Le Galop désuni du devant à gauche. *Le Galop désuni du derriere à gauche.*

114

Le Galop uni à droite.

Le Galop faux à droite

Le Galop' uni à gauche.

Le Galop faux à gauche.

L'Amble.

L'Aubin.

ALURES ARTIFICIELLES.

Airs près de terre.

Le Passage.

La Galopade.

La Volte à droite.

La Pirouette à Gauche.

Le Terre-à-terre

Le Mezair

ALURES ARTIFICIELLES.

Airs Relevez.

La Pésade.

La Courbette.

La Croupade.

La Balotade.

La Capriole.

L'AVANT-MAIN

Le Front	1
Les Temples	2
Les Salieres	3
La Ganache	4
Les Levres	5
Les Nazeaux	6
Le Bout-du-nez	7
Le Menton	8
La Barbe	9
L'Encolure	10
Le Crin ou la Criniere	11
Le Toupet	12
Le Gosier	13
Le Garot	14
Les Epaules	15
Le Poitrail	16
Le Coude	17
Le Bras	18
L'Ars	19
La Chateigne	20
Le Genou	21
Le Canon	22
Le Nerf	23
Le Boulet	24
Le Fanon	25
Le Paturon	26
La Couronne	27
Le Sabot	28
Les Quartiers	29
La Pince	30
Le Talon	31

SITUATION

EXTERIEURES

EVAL

MALADIES

DU CHEVAL

Ch. Parrocel pinx.   J. Audran Sculp.

Mr. le Comte   de St. Aignan.

Charle Partocel: pinxit

N. Dupuis sculp.

M. le Marquis   de Beauvilliers

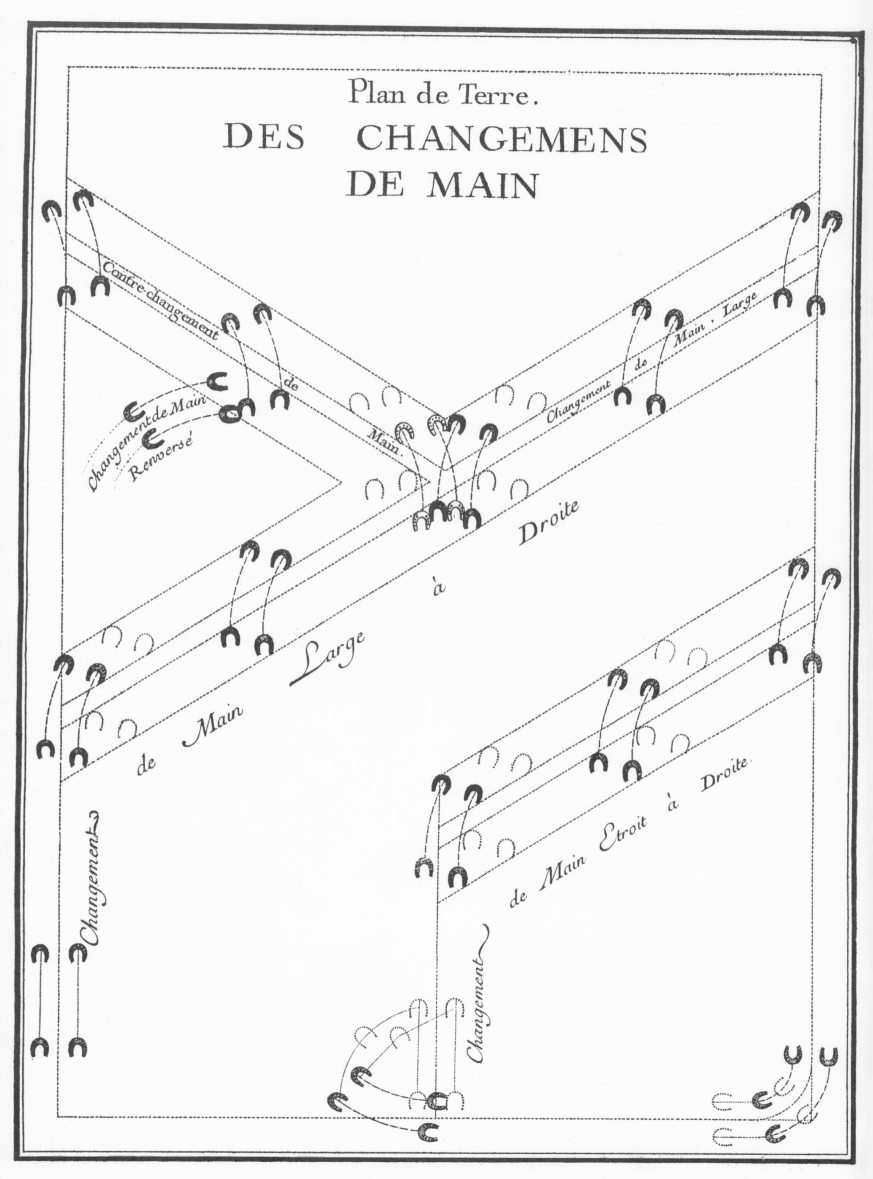

Plan de Terre.

DES CHANGEMENS DE MAIN

Contre-changement de Main.

Changement de Main Renversé

Changement de Main. Large

Droite à Large

de Main

Changement de Main Etroit à Droite

Changement

Changement

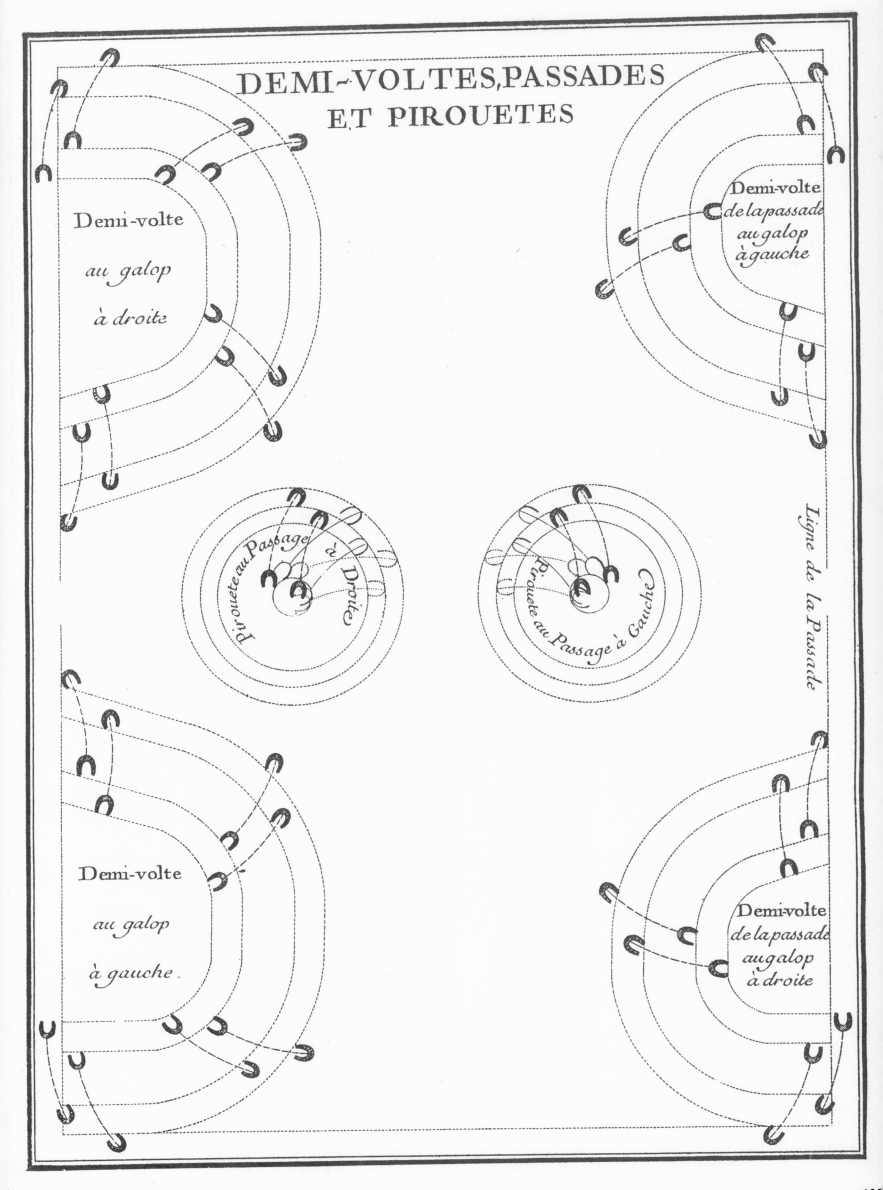

DEMI-VOLTES, PASSADES
ET PIROUETES

Demi-volte au galop à droite

Demi-volte de la passade au galop à gauche

Pirouete au Passage à Droite

Pirouete au Passage à Gauche

Demi-volte au galop à gauche.

Demi-volte de la passade au galop à droite

Ligne de la Passade

Ch. Parrocel pinx.

N. Tardieu Sculp.

l'Epaule en Dedans.

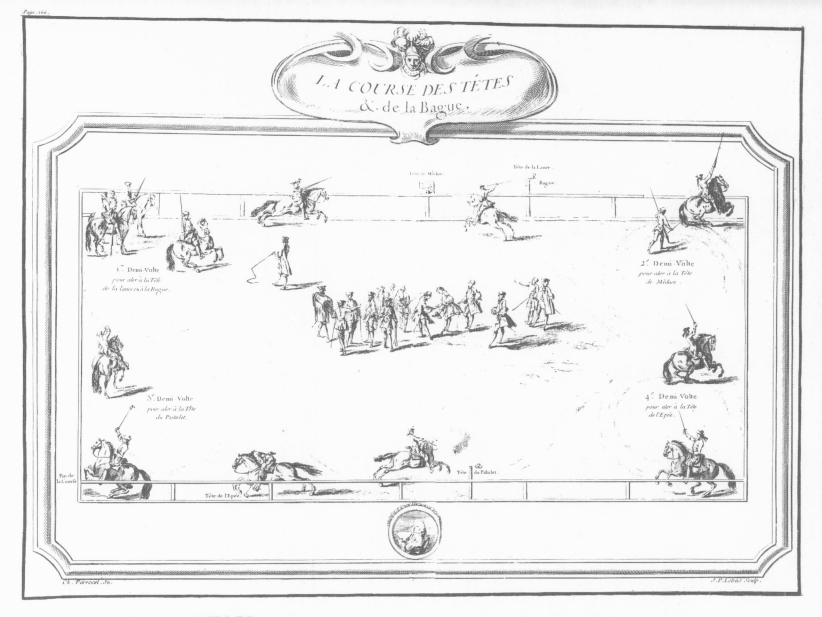

LA COURSE DES TÊTES
& de la Bague.

Tête de Méduse.

Tête de la Lance.

Bague.

1.º Demi-Volte
pour aler à la Tête
de la lance ou à la Bague.

2.º Demi-Volte
pour aler à la Tête
de Méduse.

3.º Demi-Volte
pour aler à la Tête
du Pistolet.

4.º Demi-Volte
pour aler à la Tête
de l'Epée.

Fin de
La Course.

Tête de l'Epée.

Tête & du Pistolet.

Ch. Parrocel. In.

J. P. Lebas Sculp.

LE DOUBLER.

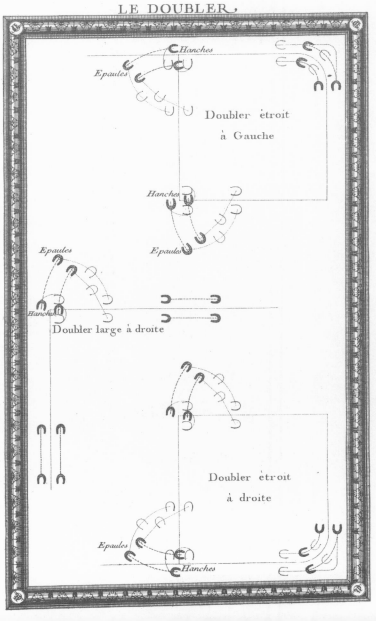

Hanches

Epaules

Doubler étroit
à Gauche

Hanches

Epaules

Epaules

Hanches

Doubler large à droite

Doubler étroit
à droite

Epaules

Hanches

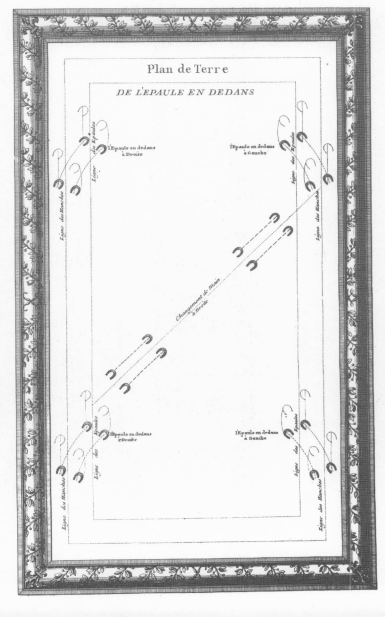

Plan de Terre

DE L'EPAULE EN DEDANS

l'Epaule en dedans
à Droite

l'Epaule en dedans
à Gauche

Ligne des Epaules

Ligne des Epaules

Ligne des Hanches

Ligne des Hanches

Changement de Main
à Droite

l'Epaule en dedans
à Droite

l'Epaule en dedans
à Gauche

Ligne des Epaules

Ligne des Epaules

Ligne des Hanches

Ligne des Hanches

127

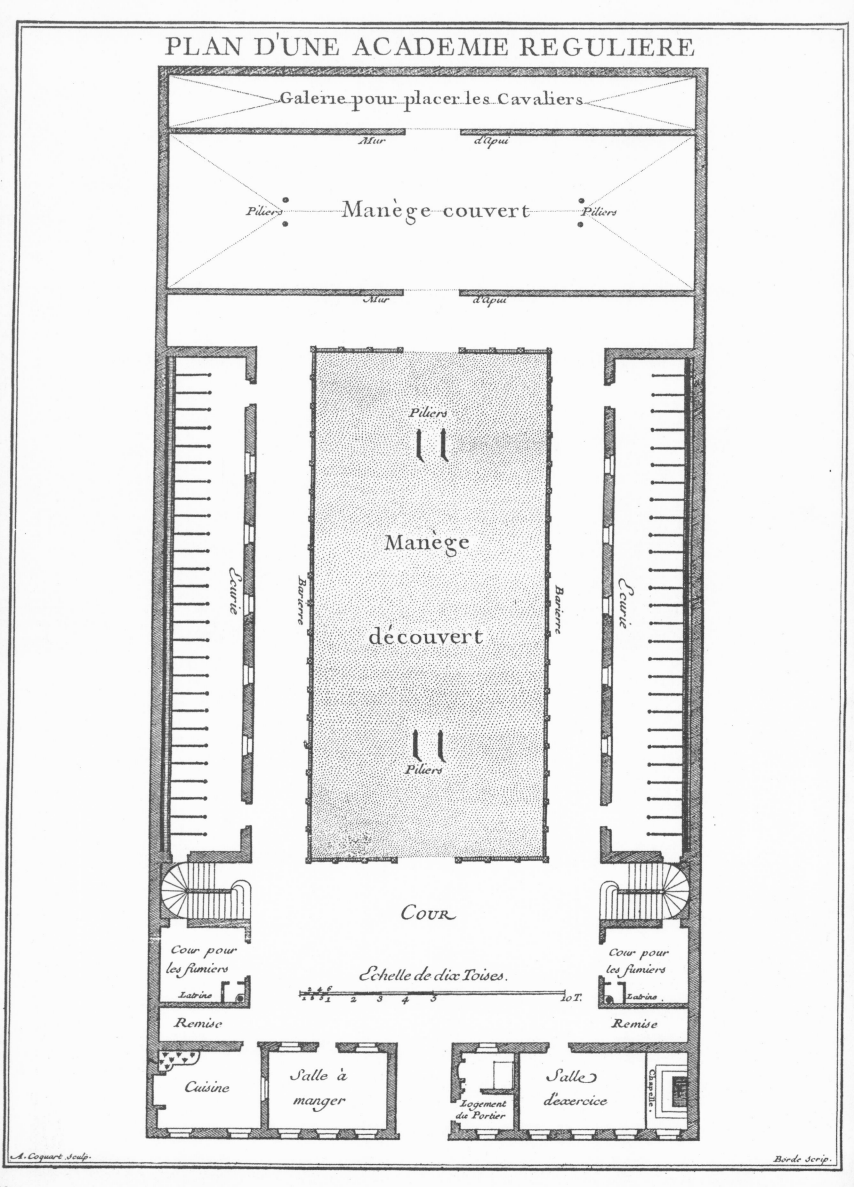

PLAN D'UNE ACADEMIE REGULIERE

Galerie pour placer les Cavaliers

Mur   d'Apui

Piliers   Manège couvert   Piliers

Mur   d'Apui

Piliers

Manège

découvert

Piliers

Ecurie   Barierre   Barierre   Ecurie

Cour

Cour pour les fumiers   Cour pour les fumiers

Latrine   Echelle de dix Toises.   Latrine

Remise   Remise

Cuisine   Salle à manger   Logement du Portier   Salle d'exercice   Chapelle

A. Coquart Sculp.   Borde Scrip.

128

HYDE PARK CORNER. 1/2 PAST 5.

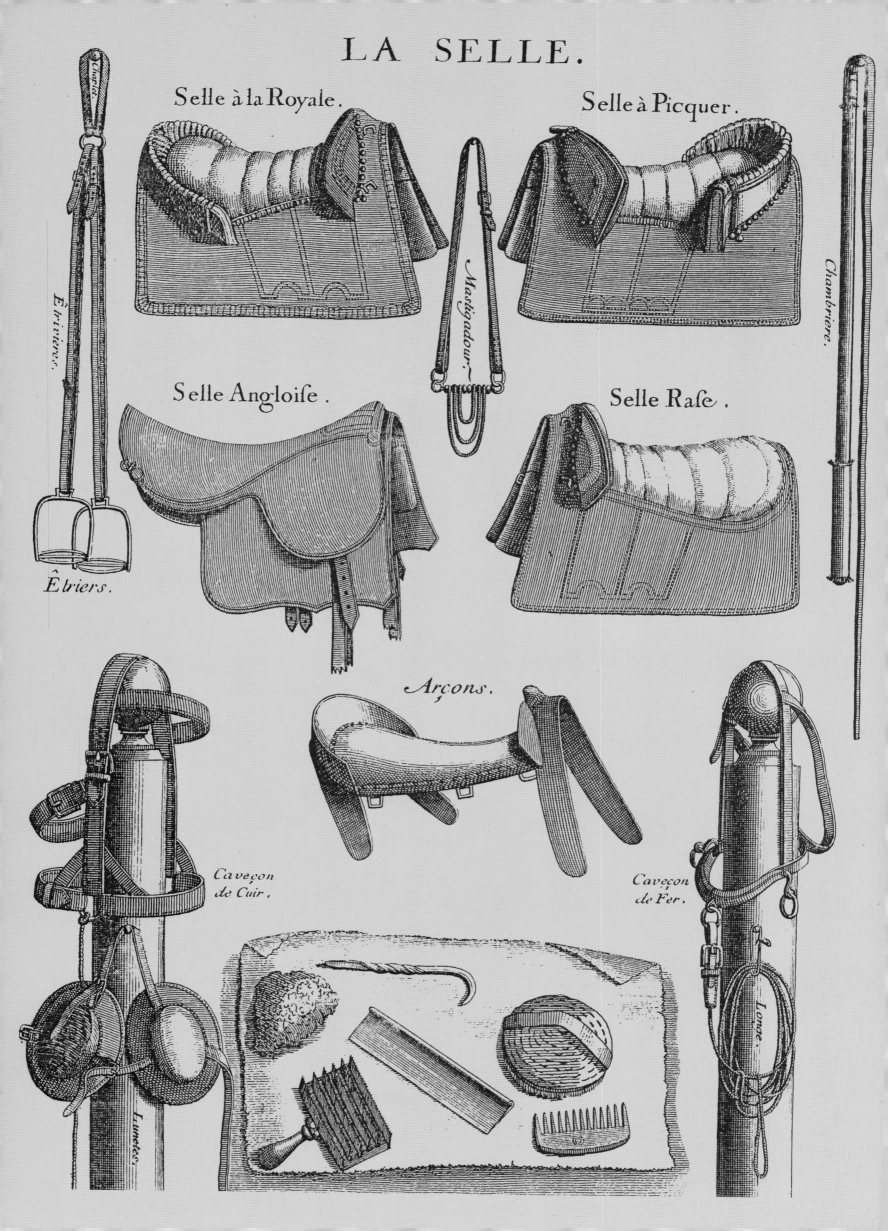

LA SELLE.

Selle à la Royale.

Selle à Picquer.

Selle Angloise.

Mastigadour.

Selle Rase.

Chaplet.

Étrivieres.

Étriers.

Chambriere.

Arçons.

Caveçon de Cuir.

Caveçon de Fer.

Lunetes.

Longe.